KEEPING
ACTIVE

To Rev. Cotton,
I hope this book
will be a help &
blessing to you.

Sincerely,
Susan Walker

KEEPING ACTIVE

*A Caregiver's Guide to
Activities with the Elderly*

· · · · · · · · · ·

Susan C. Walker

ADVISORY PANEL

Nancy DeBolt, A.C.C.
Phyllis Foster, A.C.C.
Sr. John Antonio Miller
Ruth Perschbacher, A.C.C.
Marian Smith
Robbyn Wacker, Ph.D.

 AMERICAN SOURCE BOOKS

Lakewood • Colorado

Copyright © 1994 by Susan C. Walker

Cover photo by Cindy McIntyre

ATTENTION ORGANIZATIONS AND CORPORATIONS:
This book is available at quantity discounts on bulk purchases for educational, business, or sales promotional use. For further information, please contact American Source Books/Impact Publishers, Inc. P.O. Box 1094, San Luis Obispo, CA 93406 (Phone: 1-800-2-IMPACT).

Library of Congress Cataloging-in-Publication Data

Walker, Susan C.
     Keeping Active : a caregiver's guide to activities with the elderly / Susan C. Walker.
          p. cm.
     Includes bibliographical references and index.
     ISBN 0-9621333-7-X : $8.95
     1. Aging parents—United States—Family relationships.
2. Aging parents—Home care—United States. 3. Aging parents—Health and hygiene—United States. I. Title.
     HQ1063.6.W35   1994
     306.874--dc20   93-37323

Printed and bound in the United States of America

CONTENTS

Acknowledgments

· · · · · · · · ·

To my Heavenly Father, who sustains me through life's trials and joys, and who gave me the ability to write.

To my family, Jerry, Mark, Danae and Nadia, who continue to allow me to care for all the people I love. Thank you for understanding.

To Virginia Watts Smith, my Mom, who showed me that there are no limits to what a woman can and should do. From caring for a sick husband, to finishing college at age 45, to writing a book, and surviving a massive heart attack, you have been a picture of strength, wisdom and courage; and to my Stepdad, Dr. Donald Smith, for supporting his second family as though we were his first.

In memory of my Dad, Stan Watts, whose early life of freely giving to others, bravery through the trials of Lou Gehrig's Disease, and death at 41, influenced me toward service.

For her unfailing support of me as a person, and of my constant stream of new ideas, her attention to all the details for which I can never find the time, and her careful and constructively critical reading of this manuscript, I thank my co-worker and friend, Linda Johnston.

To Phyllis Foster and Marion Smith, friends and mentors to me, and to activity professionals everywhere, for their thoughtful review and editorial comments, my heartfelt thanks. Thanks, Phyllis, for recommending that I consider writing this book.

To Dr. Robbyn Wacker and Dr. Karen Roberto of the Masters in Gerontology Program at the University of Northern Colorado, thank you for making me question my assumptions about aging, and for challenging me to academic excellence.

To Steven Phillips, my publisher, appreciation for his excitement about this topic, and his outstanding and patient editorial support.

Finally, to the Board and staff of the Seniors' Resource Center of Jefferson County, Colorado; and especially to the wonderful staff, participants and caregivers of the DayBreak Adult Day Program, this book is for you. Thank you for giving me a reason to write.

INTRODUCTION

· · · · · · · · ·

Keeping Active is a book about living. It's not just about "special activities" like going out to eat, concerts, walks, dancing, or attending church; it also helps the caregiver arrange the day and the environment in such a way that both the caregiver and the care receiver feel as happy and as normal as possible. From brushing teeth, to dressing, to going out for lunch, to caring for personal bathroom needs, the caregiver supports the care receiver in maintaining skills, living life to the fullest, and remaining active. The book also shows the caregiver how to build on strengths, and yet face losses in the person for whom they are providing care.

A QUICK TOUR

This book addresses the needs of elderly people who are moving in the direction of, or already experiencing, noticeable physical and/or cognitive loss. Here is a quick tour of what is covered, chapter by chapter:

In Chapter 1, you will learn how to assess your parent's level of activity, and when and how to assist them in being more (or less) active.

With that information at hand, you can help create an activity plan that works for both you and the person for whom you provide care. Chapter 2 shows you how to make a plan of activity built on your parent's past, his or her present desires, and on strengths that remain today.

In Chapter 3, you are introduced to community resources and activities that support you and your parent in the quest to remain active. Chapter 4 offers insight into activities and events that involve children and others outside your parent's age group. It presents you ideas on planning for successful intergenerational exchanges.

Confusion and memory loss, expected to affect approximately 50 percent of the population 85 and over in the form of Alzheimer's disease or multi-infarct (small stroke) dementia, are discussed in Chapters 5 and 6. These two chapters help you understand memory loss and confusion, and supply you with techniques and approaches that assist you and your confused parent through the many activities of the day.

In Chapter 7, we look closely at the areas of physical and sensory loss. Maximizing remaining strengths is emphasized, through the rearrangement of living environments and other adaptations.

Chapter 8 aids the caregiver in pursuing options for care outside the home, when it is no longer possible for you, the home caregiver, to support an ongoing active life for the care receiver alone. In-home help, day programs, and various types of residential living are defined and reviewed.

WHO NEEDS THIS BOOK?

The person presently committed to home care will perhaps benefit first and foremost from the information found herein. It is the person experiencing caregiving on a daily basis that will be the most likely to relate to the scenarios and suggestions offered. However, families that feel they are progressively moving from offering occasional assistance mowing lawns or providing travel to the doctor, to more consistent and time-consuming caregiving responsibilities, may find that the book provides sound suggestions for addressing future caregiving issues.

Though the focus of this book is toward family caregiving situations, professional caregivers such as CNAs, nurses, activity professionals, and social workers may also benefit.

While you may think that you do not yet need a book on keeping your elderly loved one active, you may want to reconsider. Learning as much as you can now about what may lie ahead, and putting together a solid, though flexible plan of action, will make all the difference in the world if and when a full-blown caregiving situation arises in the future.

THE BALANCING ACT: LOSSES VS. STRENGTHS

In this book I have tried to emphasize the importance of striking a balance between building on the strengths the elderly person still has and recognizing and dealing honestly with losses, and the pain they cause both caregiver and care receiver. Oftentimes activities professionals, gerontologists, and other professional caregivers play down the losses people inevitably experience as they get older in order to concentrate their efforts on building on strengths. But you, as primary caregiver, have spent many years with your aging loved one, and cannot easily brush aside the issue of loss. Also, the progressive nature of loss may have left its toll on you, as it has on many caregivers, leaving you anxious, depressed, or in complete denial that any problems exist.

How should the caregiver look at the issue of loss versus strength? Should more attention be paid to what physical and mental powers remain rather than what has been lost? How can you set an activity and caregiving course based on a realistic, yet hopeful, view of the future, both for the person you are caring for and for yourself? *Keeping Active* is intended to help you answer these tough questions.

YOUR PARENT, OR SOMEONE ELSE?

For convenience I use "your parent," "Mom," or "Dad" in this book to identify the person who is receiving care. Although many people reading *Keeping Active* are indeed caring for elderly parents, there are other readers who are caring for a spouse, grandparent, aunt or uncle, or even a close friend. The information that follows is just as useful for these caregivers as it is for those who are caring for aging parents. So, as you read the book, if it helps, replace "your parent" with the correct name for your older relative and friend, and rest assured that the information provided applies equally well to your caregiving situation.

A FINAL WORD . . .

It is not the intent of this book to suggest that all, or even a majority, of older people suffer major losses. Instead, it is written for the minority of aging people who have suffered significant losses and for the people who are responsible for their care. In spite of this book's emphasis on helping the caregiver help the care receiver, the intent of that assistance is to enable the care receiver to remain as independent as possible for the longest possible time. The person for whom you care should be a co-decision maker as long as he or she is able.

It is my desire that *Keeping Active: A Caregiver's Guide to Activities with the Elderly* will assist you and the person for whom you care in maintaining the best possible quality of life. As you will see in the pages that follow, a full, active life for your aging loved one will be firmly rooted in acknowledging losses and at the same time building on remaining strengths, thus allowing you to make a workable activity plan.

It is up to us, as caregivers, to assist in keeping the human spirit alive and active in those for whom we care. Best of luck on your journey!

Chapter One

ASSESSING ACTIVITY LEVELS

· · · · · · · · ·

"I know Mom's losing weight, and her neighbor's been concerned that she's not eating. Mom used to be so neat and clean—now she wears the same dress every day. She doesn't keep house much anymore, and she seems anxious about everything. She always walked a lot, and was never without a good book. I haven't seen her with a book for months, and she's afraid to leave the house. I don't want to interfere, but I'm really worried about her."

—Joanne, nurse, age 47

IT'S NOT UNUSUAL FOR A WORKING CAREGIVER TO WORRY about changes in an aging parent's level and pattern of activity, but making a good decision about whether your parent is active enough is hard to do. How do you know if encouraging increased activity levels is the right thing to do, or if keeping your mom or dad busy just makes you feel better?

Aging parents with physical or mental impairments sometimes seem to choose to be inactive. Arthritis, cancer, or diabetes can cause discomfort and pain that make mom appear perfectly happy just to sit in front of the TV. Grieving over the loss of a spouse or not being able to drive anymore can lead to sleeping most of the day. Confusion and forgetfulness can make it difficult for you mother to finish tasks that were once easy to do. A recent broken hip can make it hard for her to be on her feet.

Generally, it is important that your parent's life continue to have balance. A good rule of thumb is to observe whether she is sleeping a lot more than she is awake, or sitting or lying down a majority of the time. Encouraging a healthy mix of activities based on her functioning level (what she is able to do) is appropriate. Assist and encourage your parent to divide her time between rest, daily maintenance and hygiene activities, interactions with peers and other individuals, exercise, private time, and a host of other activities that are right for her.

Life and activity go on in spite of your aging parent's physical or cognitive losses. To you it may feel as if Mom's productive days are over, but with the help of a modified life activity plan and support from family and friends, many elders with losses continue to enjoy life. You can help by providing daily opportunities for the most normal, ongoing life experiences possible. A caregiver recently considering our adult day program told me that she was taking her husband, who had Alzheimer's disease, on several trips, and enrolling him and the family in an early- stage Alzheimer's discussion/support group. She recognized the need to continue to involve him in familiar, ongoing life activities, such as social/support gatherings and trips that they both loved before he became ill.

In this chapter, you will discover some ideas to help you organize and understand what activities can be undertaken with an elderly person experiencing physical or cognitive losses, some thoughts on humor and its place in helping both the caregiver and care receiver through the day's activities, and how to conduct an activity assessment to see whether the the elderly person is staying appropriately involved in the world around her.

THINGS WE DO DAILY

We do not think about it much, but for most of us several different kinds of activities make up the day. When we are functioning in a healthy way, both physically and cognitively, life often seems to run itself. As functioning levels change, it is important to carefully analyze the makeup of a day. Here is an easy way to look at all the things we do that are part of our everyday experience.

√ THINGS WE HAVE TO DO

These are things like eating, sleeping, and going to the bathroom. If we want to live healthy, happy lives, it is important to do these activities on a regular schedule.

√ THINGS WE SHOULD DO

Another aspect of staying healthy and happy includes doing lots of little things every day, like brushing our teeth, combing our hair, bathing, dressing, and working around the house. While we do not have to undertake these activities, doing so makes life a lot more pleasant for us and others. (Things we have to do and should do are referred to in professional care settings as ADLs, or activities of daily living.)

√ THINGS WE LIKE AND WANT TO DO

These are special activities that can be done alone, or in the company of friends and family; they happen at home or out in the community. They include reading a book, playing table games, taking trips, dining in restaurants, going to church, dancing, hiking, singing, and watching TV and movies. Even after retirement or physical and cognitive decline, many older people still get satisfaction from performing tasks reminiscent of their former employment. Volunteer activities also build confidence and raise self-esteem. When your parent participates in these activities, he or she is made to feel important and needed.

USING GAMES AND HUMOR

If your parent is slightly confused or cannot see as well as in the past, it takes longer to do the things that have to—and should—be done. Accomplishing the necessary tasks of life take so much time that there may not be much energy left to enjoy special events, or the THINGS WE LIKE TO DO. Even with your help, it may take an hour before bathing and dressing are completed. Your parent used to look forward to your weekly Sunday afternoon shopping trip together, but now such an undertaking hardly seems worth the effort to her.

Since more of your parent's time is spent on necessary activities, it sometimes helps to think of fun ways to get them done. Reminiscing with her while helping her bathe, or playing a word game while cutting her nails makes life's daily chores easier to handle while giving her something to think about.

If you spend a lot of time giving care, it is easy to lose sight of life's brighter side. Plenty of smiles, humor, and flexibility can make it all seem a little less serious, and more enjoyable. While it may seem sad that your parent is coming to the end of life, an appropriate sense of humor and lots of laughter can make the sadness bearable.

Aging parents, whether they have physical or cognitive losses (or both), like and need to be taken seriously. Well-placed humor and fun in the caregiving situation means laughing with them, while at the same time clearly showing them the respect they deserve.

WHY AN ACTIVITY ASSESSMENT IS DONE

There are important reasons to invest some time in looking at how your parent is keeping active. Here are a few:

- A review of Mom's life and activity patterns brings you "up to date," and can be a building block for a positive, ongoing caregiver/care receiver relationship.

- Taking the time to identify and focus on Mom's strengths, interests, and present activity patterns helps you to be more positive, and perhaps more objective, as the two of you try to work with any existing losses.

- Being pro-active and doing something is usually better than doing nothing. Think of reviewing activity levels as identifying where you and your parent are on the "caregiving map." Knowing your starting point helps you a lot in determining what direction to undertake.

- Assessing life activity patterns is an important step in making an activity plan (see Chapter Two). Some planning makes the day, and life in general, go more smoothly.

MAKING AN ACTIVITY ASSESSMENT

Assessing activity levels sounds very technical, but it is really just a way of saying, "I need to take a look at where my parent is right now, and how we can work together to ensure the best possible present and future." Taking the time to do an inventory of your parent's present strengths, losses, sleeping, eating, and general activity patterns (with her if possible, based on present abilities) can positively influence levels of life satisfaction and personal self-esteem. Doing this not only helps the person you are caring for, but it assists you in making any mental adjustments necessary in accepting the new person your parent is, or is becoming. In the case of stroke or Alzheimer's disease, for instance, a huge adjustment to a very different person than you once knew is often necessary.

Activity directors in nursing homes, retirement centers, day programs, and senior centers make professional activity assessments every day. Where has the resident or participant been in life, and where is he or she now? What are his or her basic human functioning needs in physical, spiritual, social, cognitive and emotional areas? What strengths and interests does he or she have that can be built on? What losses need to be considered while making an activity plan that promotes success and esteem enhancement? These are the kinds of questions activity directors address when designing their activity plans. Your assessment will not be quite as technical as theirs, but it will work just as well!

Your activity assessment should include the following considerations and tasks:

Consideration

First, remember that healthy aging includes some slowing of mind and body. Part of making sense out of life for Momis taking long looks back to see where she has been. Sometimes looking back is best done from a comfortable chair—it may seem boring and not very active to you, but it can be an appropriate activity for an elderly parent, as long as it is not the only activity that she undertakes. While the present and future offer joy and fulfillment for your parent, much life satisfaction will be derived from remembering the past. Allow adequate time for solitude, and one-on-one conversations regarding important past events.

Task 1

Keep track of approximately how much time is spent each day in rest and sleep.

Task 2

Talk with your parent to gather as much direct information from her as possible regarding past and present interests and strengths, and her need and desire to be active and productive.

Consideration

See if Mom's present life activities look anything like they used to. Does she still take walks? Is a paperback book open on the coffee table? A major change in her lifestyle could be a warning sign that things are not the way they should be.

Task

Schedule a physical examination and based on the physician's assessment of health and general well being, make a list with your parent of all the activities you can think of that need to be part of the day.

Consideration

Getting input from a variety of people who have known your parent may help to confirm or deny your feeling that things have changed, and some intervention needs to be considered.

Task

Talk with family, friends, and neighbors who have known your parent for a long time, and get their observations on any changes in her activity pattern. Sharing your concerns with professionals who work with aging people can be helpful, too.

Consideration

It is often challenging to make a decision with or for someone that will affect change in their lives. The challenge is usually achievable if you have followed the steps presented here.

Task

Make a decision based on all the information you gather to assist Mom in becoming more active, maintaining current level of activity, or, if necessary, helping her adjust to a lower activity level.

It is easier and faster for you to do some of the things your parent used to do, but taking over too early can create dependence on you and make your life more difficult than it needs to be. For example, Mom may not do dishes as thoroughly as she used to, and her hair may not be as tidy as it once was, but permitting her to care for these things as long as possible allows her to stay productive and keep her dignity.

Activities with which Mom may or may not need assistance will vary based on her own particular situation. Some people can dress themselves, but may need help with buttons. Others with cognitive challenges may need help in choosing appropriate clothing to wear. A parent with stroke or arthritis may have trouble combing his or her hair because they have to raise their arms above their shoulders, but they may be able to brush their teeth easily. Common sense should be your guide as you choose where to assist and where to support Mom's independence.

Some activities your parent does could be dangerous, and depending on what kinds of problems she is having, you should step in to help when necessary. Some examples of dangerous activities are:

- getting in and out of the bathtub if physically frail
- driving if eyesight is poor
- using the stove or having access to sharp knives and scissors if confused and forgetful
- crossing a busy street to get to the store if hearing is gone.

Put yourself in Mom's shoes, and treat her as you would like to be treated in a similar situation. Don't feel guilty for being there to lend support when you need to be, but let her do for herself (and for you!) when she can.

If the elderly person for whom you are caring has been home alone for a long time and has stopped seeing friends, it might take some hard work on your part to convince her that she needs to find some things to do. It may be perfectly clear to you that getting out of the house for dinner would make your parent feel better, but it may not be clear to her at all. Do not forget that none of us is totally comfortable the first time we visit a new place, or try out something we have not done before. It takes time, patience, and support to help someone you love get excited about life a second time around.

THINGS TO DO

√ Talk with an activity professional at a local day program or care facility, and find out how they assess the activity needs of the people they serve. Most activity professionals would be pleased to spend time talking with you at little or no charge. Be aware that they are extremely busy people, so be sure to make an appointment ahead of time.

Since you may eventually want to consider an adult day program to supplement your "at home" caregiving activity plan, use this consultation time to evaluate whether you and your parent could both benefit from using the program's services a couple of days each week.

√ Check with your parent's regular doctor or geriatric physician specialist to get his or her opinion as to how much and what kind of activity is good for her. While you are there, have her undergo a complete medical work-up and evaluation. In both day programs and care facilities, a physician must indicate in writing how much activity is good for the patient. While you do not need this information in writing for your home activity plan, your physician's recommendation will help you set up the fullest plan possible for your parent.

√ If you are working with a geriatric care (or case) manager, talk with them about your parent's activity levels and pattern as part of her overall care picture. Depending on your care manager's background, he or she may be qualified to discuss activities with you or refer you to an activities professional or recreation therapist. If you are not currently working with a geriatric care manager, you can expect consultation fees to range between $40 and $60 per hour.

√ Take a work lunch hour to list your parent's areas of strength and those in which she has suffered losses. Do this first from your perspective alone. You will need to sit down later and make a similar list with her. This list helps you take a good look at how to assist her in arranging her day so that she can accomplish the things that have to be done, the things that should be done, and the special things she has a choice about doing.

√ Go to your local library and check out *The Feeling Great Wellness Program for Older Adults* by J. Weiss. It provides a way of measuring how well your parent is really doing at staying healthy and active. Look for other books on health and wellness while at the library.

√ Ask the reference librarian to help you find books and articles on recreational opportunities for the elderly, or on leisure in general. Local recreation districts also offer free booklets on classes and trips especially designed for seniors.

√ Get a spiral notebook, and begin a list of activity ideas. Become a watchful "activities detective," drawing from your parent's former favorite pastimes. Also, talk with her neighbors, friends, and other family members, and consult newspapers, TV, magazines, and books to discover ways to help your parent meet daily activity needs and desires.

√ Call nearby college libraries until you find one that has a subscription to the professional journal *Activities, Adaptation & Aging*. Visit the library and thumb through several volumes to familiarize yourself with the issues that activities professionals deal with on a daily basis.

Chapter Two

MAKING AN ACTIVITY PLAN

. . . .

"Since Dad's illness, life has been difficult. It's the busiest time of the year at work, and Dad requires constant attention. I used to have a social life, but lately I'm lucky if I get to the Y once a month to play racquetball. It's all so overwhelming. Most of the time, I don't know what to do next."

—*Steve, Marketing Director, age 45*

As with most caregivers, your schedule is probably very full. Juggling home responsibilities, your parent's care, and possibly a career may leave little free time for your needs.

Because you have so much to get done and cannot spend all your free time with your parent, planning is crucial. While most days will not be perfect, you will find that a little planning helps things go more smoothly. Making an activity plan for you and Dad organizes your day so you can accomplish what you need to do and still have a little time for yourself.

This chapter starts out by exploring some ways to keep you, the caregiver, organized. It then shows you how, in spite of Dad's losses, to build on his strengths, and to use pleasant memories from his past to create an activity plan for today.

Finally, the chapter offers a realistic look at your parent's activity limitations, and then shows you how to put everything together to make a successful activity plan. As you read this chapter, be aware that your ability to organize yourself will have a big impact on how well you and your parent work together.

PLANNING AS A CAREGIVING TOOL

A loose definition of planning might be "charting a course for the future based on a careful review of past experience, a close look at present circumstances, and your best guess as to what the future may bring." Caregivers must organize a plan that allows a great deal of flexibility.

Having a planned schedule at our day program that includes two meals and at least four group activities helps us through the day with 35 to 40 confused, wheelchair bound, blind, or otherwise challenged participants. We allow plenty of room in that plan for surprises, such as a drop-in participant or two; an unexpected birthday or other special event in one of our participant's lives; or one-on-one needs, such as walking outside with a wanderer, and reassuring an anxious participant about what time they will be going home.

As a caregiver, you will also experience surprises in your day. Some will be pleasant, others will not. Being flexibly organized provides you structure, but allows give and take when it is needed.

Here are some good reasons for you and your parent to get organized with an activity plan:

- Letting events fall where they may could mean that a lot of really important things will not get done. A good example of this is exercise. If we do not designate a special time each day for exercise, it most often does not happen.
- Making an activity plan, or a plan for getting through the day, gives you and your parent something to work on together, and may deepen and improve your relationship.

- Investing time in chatting about the past and present, as well as together anticipating the future, sends a clear message to your parent that you care.
- Good planning helps to bring about order, and order is an ongoing essential part of all life as we know it. When you and your parent begin a joint care venture, at least two people who have lived relatively separate and self-directed lives sometimes suddenly find themselves more bound together in an interdependent situation. Making these two lives gel demands planning. A quick recording on paper of what your day looks like, and alongside it what your parent's day looks like, will give you some idea why planning is so necessary if you hope to get things done.

GETTING ORGANIZED

Getting organized takes time, but it is time well spent. Remember that investing now in planning will pay off with more successful days in the future. A simple formula may be helpful to get you started:

P ⇒ Prioritize
L ⇒ List
A ⇒ Act
N ⇒ Network

Prioritize

You have heard the old saying, "Don't put off till tomorrow what you can do today." In today's fast-paced world, many of us take that statement very literally and try to squeeze more into today than it can possibly hold. Start your planning adventure by looking at one of the prioritizing systems on the market; *DayTimer®* has an excellent one. Or you can experiment with designing your own system.

If you decide to design your own system, give tasks to be accomplished a rating according to their level of urgency.

You could use simple ratings, such as Level 1, Level 2, and Level 3. Anything at Level 3 gets done only when all your Level 1 and 2 activities are completed. Think through the things that need to be accomplished for the day, and prioritize them in your mind. Here's an example:

- Pay bills — Level 1
- Buy dog food — Level 1
- Make flight reservation for business trip — Level 2
- Make a few calls re: in-home help for Dad — Level 2
- Drop off clothes at cleaners — Level 3

You may already have an informal system of prioritizing that seems to be working well. If so, it is not necessary to change your system, or to make it more complicated. As your parent's care load increases, you may find it necessary to adjust your system somewhat, or to adopt a new one to accommodate increased demands placed on your time.

List

While it is great to prioritize in your mind, writing down your daily tasks and special activity ideas enhances the planning process, and makes it easier for you to accomplish what you set out to do. Remember that putting your ideas and goals on paper and checking them off as you get them done helps you be more accountable and efficient.

There are several ways to organize your day on paper. You may find that one way works better for you than another. Here are some ideas to try. Experiment with them, and see if one of them works for you.

- Plan with a list that progresses through the day from morning to evening. If you use a "Weekly Minder" calendar at work, you are already used to this system.
- Try organizing your day by making two lists, things to do at the office, and things to do at home (or things to do at home, and things to do at the nursing home, or board and

care, if your parent lives in one). For some people, this is the most logical and practical way to organize the day.

- Another way to list things to do is to simply list them in order of importance.

As you do your lists each day, you will notice that they start to fall into a pattern. Being aware of patterns may eventually make your planning much easier. Much of what we do each day is repetitive, and can go on a basic list that may look much the same each day. Activities to be added to the basic list could include doctor appointments, plays or movies, hikes, and special projects of various kinds. Taking the time to capture thoughts about the day on paper and organize those thoughts into lists, moves you a step closer to getting everything done.

Act

Once you have decided what really needs to be done on a daily basis, do it! Prioritizing in your mind and making lists on paper are important, but will not mean much if you do not follow through with action.

A good way to check yourself to see exactly what you have accomplished is to keep your lists in your notebook, and mark off tasks as you complete them. At the end of the week, it is rewarding to look back and see exactly what you have been able to get done.

Network

Attempting to accomplish all your tasks by yourself is nearly impossible. Accomplish a lot with less effort by tapping resources and people around you. Following are some networking ideas to try:

- *Carpool.* Not only does this provide you the opportunity to save gas and wear and tear on your car, but you have time to exchange ideas with your fellow carpoolers.

- *Meet new people.* Expose yourself to new friends who will challenge you with different ways of looking at the world.
- *Renew old friendships.* Acquaintances from the past can provide expertise in areas where you have little or none. Their insight may help you solve a problem or complete a project in half the time it would take you to do it yourself.
- *Visit libraries and other resource centers often.* The more information you have at hand when facing dilemmas, the more quickly and easily they will be solved.

Now that we have reviewed some simple principles for keeping you organized, let us look at your parent's past life and present functioning level to identify some ways to successfully enhance his daily activities.

COLLECTING MEMORIES

Reminiscing is an important later-life activity. Faced with less years ahead, older adults like your parent find pleasure and life significance in reviewing the past. Reminiscing activities help your parent make sense of where he has been and provides a reservoir of memories that can be used to build an activity plan with him today.

Start by making a list of pleasant memories from your childhood. Chances are you spent many happy moments with your parent. What kinds of things did he plan for those special days you shared? Fishing? Watching a ball game? Maybe a high spot for the two of you was smiling at each other as you devoured Mom's Sunday pot roast.

Next, take Dad on a walk down memory lane. An old photo album, or letters received from a friend or lover can help to start the memories flowing. Work together to create a list of jobs and hobbies that your parent enjoyed. Was he a pilot during the war? Did he build model planes? His losses may make it hard for him to do everything he once loved to do, but remembering is fun, and should help to produce some activity ideas that can be adapted to meet his current physical and cognitive ability level.

Activity plans in day programs and care facilities grow out of extensive conversation between the activities director and the resident/participant, and similar conversation with family members and friends. Activity professionals use a list of questions to stimulate conversation in the person they are getting to know. What they learn helps them plan activities that meet the needs and desires of the people they serve.

While it isn't necessary for you to work from such a list at home with your own parent, it may be helpful for you to see some of the questions activity professionals ask. Here are some sample questions from a day program:

- What is your previous occupation?
- What is your favorite food?
- What is your favorite color?
- What hobbies do you enjoy?
- What is your happiest family memory?
- What is your favorite animal?
- Did you have pets when you were growing up? Do you remember their names?
- What season of the year do you like the best? Why?
- Which of the following activities do you enjoy? Church, bingo, cards, swimming, movies, reading, knitting, music, watching television, dancing?

Be aware that for people with confusion and memory loss, questions should be asked in such a way so that only a yes or no answer is required. Many confused people will not be able to answer your questions in whole sentences, and may not be able to find the right word to express what they want to say. Try asking the question about favorite seasons this way: "Do you enjoy spring?" After you are given the answer you can ask, "The leaves are beautiful, aren't they?" Asking yes-no questions offers the person with dementia a chance to succeed in conversation, and allows him to participate in the making of his activity plan.

ANOTHER LOOK AT FUNCTIONING LEVELS

Besides questions about favorite activities from the past and present, activity professionals also need to know something about levels of functioning. Much of this information is available in the medical chart at the nursing home or day program. Some of it is gained just by observing the resident or participant over time.

Being aware of losses helps activity professionals focus on strengths that remain. They then work with their participant/resident to build a realistic activity plan. You need to make a similar assessment at home with your parent. Dad's level of physical and cognitive functioning affects the amount of time the two of you schedule for each of his daily activities.

Take a careful look at your parent's routine around the house. Does he get winded easily when he exerts energy? Is he taking care of chores? Do his clothes look neat and clean? Has he bathed and washed his hair recently? Does he complain that he cannot see the TV? Do you notice that he plays the radio extra loud?

Once you have a good feel for his activity levels and abilities, try to identify ways for him to be as active as possible based on his strengths, or on what he can still do. He may love going shopping for the holidays; to help him get around try using a wheelchair or electric cart if necessary. Assist him in hearing the TV by offering him amplifying head gear, or the chair nearest the set.

Be sure to look at whether your parent is able to successfully complete those things he *has to do* and *should do*. If it looks as though he is not shampooing his hair regularly, make a point of including him in your next visit to the hair salon. You will save time and trouble by caring for both his and your hair care needs at once.

It is important for your parent to care for his own activities of daily living as long as possible. Purchasing comfortable sweats or other clothing without buttons allows your arthritic parent to dress with greater ease. Laying out a set of clothing in the morning helps your confused parent by limiting clothing choices, and reduces the chance that clothing will be layered (examples are wearing three shirts, or putting underwear on over outer clothing).

Learn to recognize when Dad needs to stay home and rest. An occasional rest is important, and should be encouraged unless it becomes his main activity. Sleeping too much might indicate that your parent is depressed or physically ill. Talk to his physician or another health care professional (a geriatric nurse, psychologist, or geriatric social worker) about how much rest or sleep is usually recommended for people his age.

PUTTING A PLAN TOGETHER

Before trying a sample activity plan, review the ideas presented in this chapter. The following steps should be taken to ensure success:

- Organize yourself.
- Collect memories of people, things, and events that were important to your parent in the past.
- Look carefully at your parent's physical and cognitive functioning levels, including present strengths and assets, as well as identifying areas in which he will need your support.
- Combine the above steps to produce an activity plan that is both flexible and organized.

Time is a major factor for both of you in planning the day's activities. Everything your parent does takes longer now—from eating, to getting in the car, to caring for personal hygiene. Your parent may not share your same sense of urgency or level of ability when it comes to getting on with the day's next activity. Thinking and planning ahead to avoid time crises makes it more likely that the day will be pleasant and fulfilling.

What are your favorite activities? Your parent may have the same interests, or they may be different. Be sure to cater to his preferences often when making activity plans.

Arrange for Dad to spend some time with peers. Mutual experiences from the early and middle 1900s may give rise to avid conversation. Include him in your activities if they are appropriate for his level of physical and cognitive functioning. It is important, though, to leave some time for him to relax in his favorite chair, while you go to the Y or jog with a friend. Remember that while it is good for you to spend time with your parent, you will both be happier having short "vacations" from each other.

THINGS TO DO

√ Go to your nearest office supply store to look at a *Day-Timer®* or other organizational system. Evaluate whether your current plan for staying organized is working. Depending on what you find, buy a system to get you started on better organization, or upgrade your present system to make it work better.

√ Revive memories from the past for you and your parent by looking at old photograph albums, reading family histories and old letters, and looking over other memorabilia.

√ Spend part of the day in a wheelchair or with earplugs in your ears to better understand what it feels like to have physical and sensory losses. Listen to a tape in a language you do not speak, and sense the despair of a person trying to understand their world when brain function has been damaged or destroyed by dementia.

√ Watch videos of *Driving Miss Daisy* and *Fried Green Tomatoes* to get a moving, entertaining, and quite realistic look at the joy, privilege, responsibility, wisdom, and sadness of aging.

√ Practice putting together an activity plan based on all you have learned in the first two chapters of this book. Try it for a couple of weeks to see if it allows you to be both flexible and organized in your approach to the day's activities.

√ Read the book *Reminiscence* by Carmel Sheridan in order to help you understand the importance of your parent's tendency to "look back."

Chapter Three

STAYING ACTIVE OUTSIDE THE HOME

· · · · · · · · ·

"I'd like to take Mom out often, but sometimes it seems like more trouble than it's worth. It takes her so long to get ready, and she says and does some pretty embarrassing things in public. I can hardly make her hear me across the table when we're out to eat. Staying home seems like the best thing to do."

— *Donna, Bank teller, age 55*

IT'S EASY FOR CAREGIVING CHILDREN AND THEIR AGING parents to become isolated from others. Friends do not visit anymore, and sometimes you're too tired to get your parent ready to go out.

In spite of difficulties you may encounter, she needs to leave the house often. While enjoying the safety and comfort of her home is important, she will not get enough stimulation if home is the only thing she experiences.

After reading the first two chapters, you should have a better understanding of your parent's activity levels and abilities, and know how to help design an activity plan that addresses her daily needs and desires. This chapter emphasizes the importance of contact with the world outside the home to ensure that your parent continues to be an active participant in life.

The chapter begins by asking the question, Why go out? If your parent says she prefers to stay home, why not allow her to do so? It then discusses community acceptance of elders with losses, and helps you identify different kinds of places your parent can go to feel welcome and comfortable. Finally, the chapter talks about discounts that are available to elders, as well as volunteer programs that provide an opportunity for her to contribute to the community.

WHY GO OUT?

For the last few years, your parent may have been content to stay at home, seldom seeing anyone but you. She used to be so active, visiting with friends, volunteering at the school, and holding down a part-time job. While she says she wants to stay home, she also talks about being lonely and having nothing to do.

What causes some elders to choose to stay at home alone, when there are so many things to do and places to go? Here are some possible explanations:

- *The aging process itself.* Many elders experience a slowing of body processes and functions. The world around them is moving at an extremely fast pace. They may sense that they cannot keep up any longer, which makes them feel safer in their home, where they can better control the speed at which events happen in their surroundings.

- *Loss of self-esteem.* It is easy to think less of yourself when you experience losses. As eyesight and hearing fail, and ambulation becomes more of an effort, older people may begin to doubt their physical abilities and perhaps even their worth as human beings.

- *Depression.* If enough self-esteem is lost, depression can result. Depression often brings activity to a halt, and slows the older person down even more, making every movement an effort. In a true clinical depression, elders may stop eating, lose weight, and spend most of their time in bed.

Depression is often successfully treated, and it is wise to have your parent or loved one see a physician for an evaluation and treatment plan.

While home can and should provide a safe haven, elders will not get enough stimulation if they stay there all the time. Surrounded by the sameness of the home environment, they soon lose their connection to the outside world, and with that loss may come a decreased interest in such life activities as dressing up and personal grooming.

Trips into the community can carry your elderly relative back to earlier days, prompting special memories of Sunday dinner at the family's favorite restaurant, Saturday night dances at the VFW, and shopping trips to the farmer's market for fresh vegetables and fruit. The reminiscing that happens during and after community excursions gives elders a feeling of happiness and satisfaction. Spending time in the community also keeps them in touch with what is happening today.

Excursions stimulate the senses and encourage elders to embrace the world at a deeper level than they could by just staying at home. They may experience that world at a slower pace than they used to, but will still benefit greatly from venturing into the community.

COMMUNITY ACCEPTANCE OF ELDERS WITH LOSSES

You and Mom are eating out and suddenly she removes her dentures. You are embarrassed, wondering what people around you are thinking.

Remember that this incident seems more serious to you than it does to others. Resist the temptation to show frustration and anxiety over the incident through extreme facial and verbal expressions. Because she is your parent, you are especially vulnerable to feelings of embarrassment. If others do notice, most of them will be understanding and accepting of the behavior.

In a former position as activities coordinator for a nursing home that served a cognitively impaired population, I joined our residents on a trip to a large performing arts center. The walk up to the auditorium was full of well-dressed theatregoers expecting a regal night out. All of a sudden, an Attends® (adult pad) began to slide down the legs of one of our female residents. At the same time, there was a trickle onto the sidewalk.

A staff member quickly picked up the Attends, and we continued our walk to the theater. Once inside the theater, we gently escorted the resident to the ladies room. If anyone noticed the incident, it was not obvious.

Embarrassing? Yes, but care facility staff are used to dealing with problems like this on a daily basis. Perhaps you will never be faced with a situation as potentially embarrassing as this one. If you are, focus on quickly, but gently, getting the problem under control. This keeps you from dwelling on being embarrassed and helps Mom out of her difficult situation.

Your parent could exhibit a number of behaviors when out in public that seem inappropriate to you. Because she cannot hear, she may talk too loud. If confused, she might try to use the tablecloth as a napkin, or put sugar on everything instead of just in the coffee. She may slow down everyone else in the grocery line, taking five minutes to write a check or to get her money out of her billfold.

Here are some ways to minimize the effect her actions and behaviors in public may have on you and others:

- Accept that your parent will exhibit some behaviors that feel uncomfortable to you.
- Realize that most people around you will be concentrating so hard on matters of their own that they may not even notice the behavior.
- Do what you can to limit the chances that embarrassing situations will happen when you are out in public, for both

your sake and hers. For instance, to avoid delays in the grocery line, assist in getting her check filled out at home.

- If embarrassing situations do happen, show by your facial expression and the way you handle the situation that you love, accept, and are proud of your parent.
- Do not make your parent feel bad by laughing out loud or expressing open anger, but feel free to use a quiet chuckle or well-placed humor to get through the situation.
- Finally, relax and trust that when you need them, the majority of your fellow human beings will be there to support you with a friendly smile or helping hand.

WHERE TO GO IN THE COMMUNITY

We have discussed why it is important for your parent to leave the house and how she will be accepted when she does. Now let's identify some places she can go and things she can safely and comfortably do that meet her need to get involved in the world outside her home.

Designed with Elders in Mind

All public places today should be accessible to seniors who need care, as well as to other people who are physically or cognitively challenged. This includes government buildings and schools, as well as churches and synagogues, community centers, and such places of business as grocery or department stores. Even our oldest buildings are being upgraded to allow access to all.

Many grocery stores now have electric carts, enabling physically challenged people to shop comfortably. Wheelchair ramps and elevators are available in most community buildings. Bathrooms are generally handicapped accessible as well, as is now mandated by law in the Americans with Disabilities Act.

A good way to decide just how appropriate a certain outing may be for your parent is to visit the location you wish to take her to ahead of time. During your visit, identify seating that demands the least amount of walking. Also, find bathrooms and emergency assistance centers, and ask whether wheelchairs will be available if they are needed.

On a recent trip to a sports arena with a cognitively challenged elder, it became apparent that though there was a first aid station in our stands, there were no wheelchairs to carry the person needing the aid to the station. Make it a point to follow up trips that uncover these kinds of problems with a letter to the city council or the mayor. Let your public officials know what frustration you faced while trying to provide a fun activity for your parent. Also let them know when you have a successful community experience!

Senior and community centers often have chair lifts that help physically challenged people in and out of the swimming pool. Many offer senior aerobics or water exercise. Centers also offer trips that are specially designed to meet the more limited activity needs of many seniors.

Some places of business welcome elders by offering special senior days. A department store in our area offers shopping days exclusively for nursing home residents and other elderly and disabled people in the community. On these special days, plenty of volunteers are available to assist shoppers with each and every shopping need. If no such special programs and services for the elderly are presently available in your community, consider beginning them.

Senior Discounts

Caring for an aging parent can be expensive, which is why you need to take advantage of any discount prices you can find that support cost-effective activities. Consider these suggestions as you look for affordable things to do in the community:

- Consult senior publications or other local newspapers for advertisements of discounts for seniors to eat out, attend plays or movies, go on trips, or join health clubs or YMCAs.

- Notice as you visit a restaurant or theater whether there is a price reduction offered for people over a certain age. Usually this notice is posted in plain view near the entrance to the facility.
- Call or visit the nearest senior or community center to gather information on low-cost trips, classes, and dances. In small towns or rural areas, churches, schools, libraries, hospitals or clinics, and local business leadership, as well as VFWs, Elks, Masons, and other civic organizations may take the place of a community center or senior center as suppliers of such information.
- Watch for mailings from your physician or local merchants that tell about special discounts for seniors for flu shots, prescriptions, dry cleaning, and other services.

As Mom ages, life may seem more costly. She needs more visits to the doctor, more prescriptions, and often has to pay someone to keep her lawn and run her errands. Remember that in spite of these sometimes higher costs of aging, your parent can take advantage of many discounts that help to preserve her continued involvement in community life.

Volunteer Programs
Part of your parent's frustration with life may be that she does not feel as if she is of value to anyone anymore. There are several volunteer programs that provide seniors the opportunity to serve each other and their community in general. This is often an excellent way to help restore an older person's self-worth. Two such programs are the Retired Senior Volunteer Program and the Foster Grandparent Program. Another interesting idea being tried at several locations across the country is the Time Bank.
- *Retired Senior Volunteer Program*
  Your parent might enjoy being a volunteer. The Retired Senior Volunteer Program (RSVP) encourages seniors to

remain involved with each other and with their community. RSVP volunteers serve in nursing homes, day programs, churches, hospitals, food banks, homeless shelters, and wherever else they are needed.

Some RSVP volunteers are nursing home residents or day program participants who get joy out of serving other people with losses. In spite of the fact that your parent has trouble walking, or has experienced eyesight loss, assume that she can still be of service to others. Volunteering may be the key to getting your aging parent involved in life again.

- *Foster Grandparent Programs*
  Mom may have enjoyed being with children more than anything else in life. The Foster Grandparent Program gives her the opportunity to share once more in the joy of holding and nurturing a child.

  Variations on the foster grandparent idea are everywhere. Consider encouraging your parent to visit a neighborhood school to talk about her childhood memories, or arrange for her to share poetry she wrote in earlier years with a sixth-grade reading class.

  Congnitively impaired day program participants in Denver give their love to newborns one day each week in the nursery of a local hospital. Elders in New York rock crack and HIV babies who need someone's touch. Many seniors, including the person you are caring for, may bring just the right blend of experience and sensitivity to these caregiving situations, helping others while raising personal feelings of self-worth.

- *Time Banks.*
  The Time Bank idea sees elders as being valuable to each other. Seniors volunteer for other seniors, helping them shop, get to the doctor, and care for household chores. Later,

when they need help themselves, they can use the hours they have accumulated in the "time bank" to get assistance during their own difficult times. The time bank idea will not work for all people who have experienced losses, but some may still be able to assist others who have experienced more advanced losses.

Getting Mom out into the community is good for everyone. It helps her stay vitally involved with the world around her, and helps give your friends and neighbors a better understanding and acceptance of aging people, as well as of the aging process.

THINGS TO DO

√ Check with your local senior center or community center to find out what kinds of activities are available that meet your parent's needs. Ask them to mail you a brochure or newsletter outlining upcoming events.

√ As you visit restaurants and other local businesses, keep your eyes open for signs offering senior discounts. If none are posted, ask about such discounts.

√ To find out whether there is a Retired Senior Volunteer Program or Foster Grandparent Program in your area, contact your Area Agency on Aging, or a local resource center for seniors. If there is no senior volunteer program in your area, you may wish to look into working with others in your community to begin one.

√ Write or call Mr. Art Moss, ElderCare Coalition, 1129 Colorado Ave., Grand Junction, CO 81501, 303/244-3804, for information on the Time Bank idea mentioned earlier.

√ Free senior newsletters and other community-oriented publications can often be found at libraries, senior and community centers, and grocery stores. These publications advertise free or low-cost activity ideas for seniors.

√ Be observant as you travel around the community. Watch other caregivers as they visit local restaurants and businesses with their parent. How do onlookers respond to embarrassing situations that may occur? Be intensely aware of how you and others respond to your parent's behaviors. Do people address you or your parent? Encourage them to address your parent directly. With another caregiver, role-play appropriate responses to challenging situations that may arise when you are out with your parent.

√ Call your Area Agency on Aging to find out about senior transportation options. Transportation may be available to your parent for a donation.

Chapter Four

INTERGENERATIONAL ACTIVITIES

· · · · · · · · ·

"Mom has always loved being with younger people. She especially enjoys children. She taught school for thirty years, and enjoyed every minute of it. I wish there was a way to get Mom involved in the lives of children and young people again without tiring her out too much."

— *Mary, Switchboard operator, age 42*

PROVIDING REGULAR OPPORTUNITIES FOR AGING PARENTS TO interact with children and other younger people may cultivate a sense of well-being. Many senior adults who seldom smile actually beam when in the company of younger people, especially children.

While your parent may enjoy reminiscing with friends her own age, it's good for her to spend time with other age groups. She may prefer a living environment without younger people, but will welcome their occasional visits.

This chapter begins by reviewing some guidelines for bringing senior adults with losses together with children and other younger people. It then identifies activities that can be carried out successfully, despite the difference in participant ages. Finally, the chapter looks at where to find younger people who might enjoy interacting with your parent.

GUIDELINES FOR INTERGENERATIONAL ACTIVITIES

As your parent grows older, she may have less energy. While she may like being around younger people, she may have difficulties keeping up with the conversation and activities that surround her.

Respect the fact that everything Mom does now takes more effort and that she may be less patient than before her losses. Realize that younger people, who generally have higher energy levels, can bolster her spirits and "do her in" all at the same time.

Because Mom may have a lower tolerance level, you will need to exercise wisdom when scheduling intergenerational activities. Preparing children for what to expect is also important. You can share with them that some of the people they will be visiting with will have hearing problems, forget things, or may fall easily. Encourage them to be understanding and supportive.

Consider the following suggestions for successful activities involving more than one age group:

- *Guarantee a successful visit or activity by being aware of the activity and age group that your parent will enjoy and benefit from the most.* For a parent with visual impairment, the feeling of holding a baby may be more satisfying than attending a dance studio recital she cannot see.

- *Limit time for activities and interchanges between seniors and younger generations.* While some seniors will be able to enjoy intergenerational activities for longer periods of time, most will do better if such activities last no more than 1 to 2 hours.

- *Acknowledge that things have changed since your parent was young.* Remind children and young people to be on their best behavior, including being polite. Before the visit, remind your mother that while children dress, talk, and act differently today, they still need lots of love.

- *Encourage intergenerational experiences for Mom, even if children and young people were not a major part of her life.*

Watching children perform or enjoying a young person one-on-one can bring a sparkle to Mom's eyes, taking her back to things she enjoyed in her own childhood. If you see that her reaction to a child's presence is negative or upsetting, try a slightly older intergenerational group or another activity altogether.

- *Sample your library's collection of books on intergenerational activities.* If there are no books specifically on that subject, look for books on "activities" or "therapeutic recreation" to see if they address intergenerational issues.

- *Enlist the help of family, friends, and neighbors in planning for and locating interesting and appropriate intergenerational activities.* Because as a caregiver you are constantly challenged to be creative, it is nice to be able to ask people around you for help with intergenerational activity ideas. Pooling resources with others takes some of the pressure off you.

- *Consider a wide variety of activities as potentially beneficial to elders and younger age groups.* Some caregivers might not take a child and an elder to opening night at the area theater or performing arts center because they fear that problems will arise. Depending on the presentation and building accessibility, such fears may be unfounded; don't give up on possible activities until you have gathered the necessary facts.

- *Identify activities you and your parent did together in earlier years that may revive happy memories if repeated now in an intergenerational setting.* Picnics, holiday meals, and gardening are activities people of all ages in your family or neighborhood may have worked on together. Your parent can enjoy these activities again when they are adapted to meet her present ability level.

ACTIVITIES THAT ARE FUN FOR ALL AGES

Sometimes it is difficult to know what to do to have fun when you are trying to involve several generations. Keeping in mind the guidelines just offered, begin to plan some intergenerational activities that are sure to please. Here are some activity categories to get you started.

Eating Activities

Eating is a joyful activity that brings pleasure to all age groups. Whether you plan a picnic, a special holiday lunch or dinner, or an evening visiting your area's newest restaurant, eating puts a smile on just about everyone's face.

Use some simple precautions to ensure that special needs are taken into account when planning your food-related outing. Can the restaurant or city park be easily accessed when babies and elders are present? Are bathroom facilities located nearby? Is the location interesting enough to young children, offering the kind of food that interests them, or something to keep them occupied while they are waiting for the meal to be served? Are seating arrangements comfortable for all participating? For instance, bringing comfortable lawn chairs to a picnic for older guests makes a lot of sense.

Think ahead to avoid problems. If Mom has Alzheimer's Disease or another form of dementia, eating activities should be short and structured to relieve her from pressure situations. Expecting a parent with dementia to sit through the whole meal is often unrealistic.

Simplify your confused parent's eating area, and seat her next to you or another adult who can quietly assist with any eating problems, calming her should anxiety arise. Be prepared to walk with her. Just getting away from the group for a few minutes can be very helpful.

If your parent is sight impaired, ask your server to have the food cut up in the kitchen. Sit in a position at the table where she has the best chance to hear you and be part of the table conversation. Because taste buds lose their sharpness in aging, your parent may need more highly seasoned foods to really enjoy the meal.

Eating activities, when well planned, provide not only the pleasure of good food, but offer excellent opportunities for socialization, smiles, and fun. Be sure to plan ahead for possible problem areas. Think through the activity ahead of time and your chances of success are greatly improved.

Socialization Activities

Many different kinds of activities provide opportunities for socialization, which in itself is a great cross-generational activity.

People love to talk, and chances are your parent is no exception. Years of experiences provide plenty to talk about. Sharing the past with a grandchild or a child from the neighborhood brings delight to many elders. Aging parents also enjoy reminiscing with their grown children about years gone by.

In my childhood and young adult years, visiting with my grandmother was a joy. While stories were sometimes repetitive and long, those visits provided me with a firm base for feelings of connectedness and belonging in my present life. They are remembered with fondness, and hold a place in my heart that can be filled with nothing else.

Allow the children in your life to have similar experiences by providing them opportunities to socialize with your parent. These socialization experiences may provide the framework that sees them through difficult times later in life.

A special kind of socialization happens for many aging parents when there is a chance to be around a tiny baby. The warmth of holding someone close, the memories stirred, the smiles shared make this a most meaningful activity.

Musical Activities

Music is a great intergenerational activity because it is meaningful to almost everyone. It brings people together, speaking to the emotions and the soul. It is truly the universal language.

Use the broad appeal of music to unite the different age groups in your life. Share with children and young people the classic songs from the past that your parent will enjoy. Some modern music may also be appropriate to share with her; some she may find disturbing or offensive because of the beat or the words. Be sensitive to her desires and concerns as she listens to music.

Elementary schoolchildren near a nursing home in the Denver area learn the old songs to share with nursing home residents. Their pleasure in singing "Shine on, Harvest Moon" and "K-K-K-Katy" is obvious. My daughter, a frequent visitor at our day program, loves "Put another nickel in, in the nickelodeon, all I want is loving you and music, music, music."

Dancing to music is fun for all ages. Whether it is in your living room with grandchildren or at the senior center, it provides your parent exercise, an opportunity to reminisce, and a chance for generations to interact with one another in a close and meaningful way.

Try music as a means of self-expression for your post-stroke parent who cannot speak, and for the toddler in your life just learning to talk. Self-expression happens for both. As pleasant sounds are heard, hands and feet move in rhythm to the music and smiles appear on everyone's face.

Be sensitive to the amount of time that is appropriate for a music activity. A gentleman in our day program who believes that piano music happens for his pleasure only, comes alive while it is played but indicates clearly when he has heard enough. As a rule, children and older adults should enjoy music for short time periods, ranging from thirty minutes to an hour. As with every rule, there are exceptions.

Older adults may enjoy watching children's dance recitals or choral presentations. Try taking your parent and a teenager or young adult to see a musical theatrical presentation. While a play with only dialogue might be too complicated to hold interest, musical plays usually have light plots and the music entertains and holds attention.

Be willing to take a chance and try all types of musical activities, including those you may have thought inappropriate for elders and young people to enjoy together. You may be pleasantly surprised to find the event a smashing success.

Use music as a tool to bring together all the important people in your life. Being wise and thoughtful about the music to be presented, and making the decision with all parties involved, makes it more likely that the activity will be enjoyed.

ACTIVITIES IN THE CREATIVE ARTS

It is important for your parent to participate in creative projects, whether she creates herself or participates as a spectator. The arts, theater, drawing, writing, poetry, cooking, and many other activities provide fulfilling, creative opportunities.

Many creative activities can be enjoyed by members of all generations. When your mom was growing up, children read more than they do today. Bring out some old poetry books when children are present. Reading poetry brings back happy memories for her, and at the same time introduces today's children to its beauty and meaning. Try writing some poetry with her to further stir her creative juices.

Some modern movies are appropriate for children and for your parent. The Disney classics, for example, including such recent releases as *Beauty and the Beast*, provide an afternoon or evening of entertainment that will be enjoyed by all ages.

Spending an afternoon or evening at the theater is a great intergenerational activity, assuming that the play has been carefully picked so as to appeal to different age groups, and that seats are positioned to provide optimum visual and sound perception. Depending on the interests and maturity level of the people attending with you, a wide range of theater productions can be enjoyed.

Art projects, whether clay, painting, or making crafts of various kinds, bring pleasure and pride to young and old alike. Try visiting a nearby shopping area to see displays of dolls, clocks, jewelry, and other crafts. Your parent may enjoy taking a painting class with you, learning more about water colors, oils, or pastels, or just dabbling in art at home for fun.

Good cooking is definitely an art. Many children and young people, as well as adult children, enjoy sharing with elders through cooking. Many older adults can recall delectable recipes, but need help shopping for the ingredients, and pulling the cooking activity together.

Notice what kinds of creative projects and activities your parent likes to take part in and then plan the project so that the people and the places that appeal to her are involved. All who participate should benefit from the arts activity if it is well thought out beforehand.

FINDING INTERGENERATIONAL FRIENDS

Many times older adults are isolated. They live in senior housing, participate in recreation at senior centers, attend adult day programs, and stay in nursing homes designed mostly for the geriatric population.

Is it possible to find people who like spending time doing things with your parent's generation? The answer is yes, and the relationship that is established between young and old is usually rewarding to both. Here are some suggestions of places where you may want to look for intergenerational friends.

Schools

Schools today are looking for meaningful life experiences for their students. Many students come from backgrounds that lack the love and support that was present when extended families lived near each other.

Teachers appreciate opportunities for their students to interact with people of all ages. Your parent will also benefit greatly from activities with schoolchildren.

Try contacting the school principal, social worker, or music teacher to set up a time to talk about intergenerational activities.

Families and Friends

Whether you find intergenerational friends in your family or in your neighborhood, the effect is the same. Your parent benefits from close relationships with people of different age groups, regardless of whether or not they are family.

A former foster mother in a Denver nursing facility recently went on television, hoping to locate the girls she had "mothered" over the years. Now, dying of cancer, she found great strength and comfort in the fact that she had made a difference for over one hundred young women. Visits from these young ladies, she felt, would help her face the end of life, knowing their future lives would be better because of her involvement with them.

What greater pleasure for your parent than to warmly hold a granddaughter or a special neighbor child on her lap. Remember that touching, hugging, and the need for physical closeness continues to be important in aging.

Civic and Church Groups

Youth groups, mens' and womens' clubs, sororities, fraternities, and Rotary Clubs are all looking for ways to be involved in people's lives. Tap these groups for service projects with the person for whom you care and other older people in your community.

Many clubs and groups enjoy visiting homebound senior adults, or seniors in day programs and nursing homes. Singing Christmas carols, reading to sight-impaired elders, help-ing with nail care, or assisting with paying bills are worthwhile intergenerational activities.

Private Businesses

Many businesses encourage their employees, ranging from young adult to retirement age, to get involved in the community through volunteer programs. They put on special dinners, lead drives to get holiday presents for nursing home residents, and take elders who can no longer drive to the doctor and the grocery store. Call the major corporations or businesses in your area to ask if they have a community relations office that handles employee volunteer services.

The community is full of people who may be available to participate in intergenerational activities. Some are just wait-ing to be asked.

THINGS TO DO

√   Create age-group categories in the following way: in-fants, toddlers, elementary school age, middle school age, senior highers, young adults, and adult children. List activities under each age division that would be fun and profitable for them and for your aging parent.

√   Call a local day program, retirement center, or nursing home to find out how they utilize younger age groups for intergenerational activities. Activities directors already have contacts and ideas for activities with multiple age groups. Use their knowledge in this area to get started on your "at home" intergenerational program.

√   Think about how your parent has reacted to recent visits from people of other age groups. What can you do in the future to make such visits more successful?

√   Look in the paper for an activity that at least three genera-tions of families or friends could enjoy together. Begin making plans to attend.

√   Assess whether your parent has a favorite age group that she enjoys being with. How can you tell it is her favorite? Plan to involve her with that group as often as possible, or as often as she wishes.

√   Ask the reference librarian at a college library to help you locate journals, such as *Generations* or *The Gerontologist*, where you can look for articles that deal with caregiving and intergenerational relationships.

Chapter Five

UNDERSTANDING CONFUSION AND MEMORY LOSS

· · · · · · · · ·

"It started with little things, like not being sure what day of the week it was. I noticed that Dad didn't appear to be taking his medicine, and he wasn't sure when he had eaten last. When he stated, over the weekend, that Mom was late getting home, I really began to worry. Mom had died five years before, and Dad, at least at this moment, wasn't aware of that. It wasn't clear exactly what was happening, but I knew I needed to talk with someone who might have some answers."

—*Marsha, age 51, teacher*

IT HAS BECOME OBVIOUS THAT YOUR DAD DOES NOT REMEMBER as well as he used to. The question is whether his forgetting and confusion are signs of normal aging, or if they indicate a more serious medical condition. Normal aging for your parent might mean that he remembers going to a movie but not the title. If he has more serious confusion and memory problems, he may not remember going to the movie at all.

Take some time to think about his behavior over the last few years. Things you might have thought only peculiar when they happened may now fit clearly into a pattern of progressive memory loss and confusion. Learning all you can about your parent's problems is an important first step in providing the support he needs. Begin your education by discussing your concerns with a physician.

This chapter shows you how to find physicians and other health care professionals who can help with a diagnosis. You will also be given some suggestions on how to get a better understanding of Dad's world by viewing it through his eyes, how to approach him to gain his cooperation, whether or not his activity levels are likely to change over time, and what to do to adjust his environment to ensure his safety and maximum activity level.

THE DEMENTIA DIAGNOSIS

It is important for you to understand why your parent forgets, because some kinds of confusion and forgetting can be reversed. Reversible causes of confusion include depression, confusion caused by medications, and changes in the level of oxygen supplied to the brain. Alzheimer's disease, multi-infarct dementia, Pick's Disease, Binswanger's Disease, and a few others are irreversible.

Physicians who specialize in diagnosing people who have memory loss and confusion include geriatricians, neurologists, and psychiatrists. For a holistic review of Dad's situation, seek out a physician who works with a team in a senior health center setting. Here, nurses, social workers, and a health care team work with the doctor to identify physical, cognitive, and psychosocial problems that may be present.

If the health care team evaluating your parent is unfamiliar with his past and recent medical history, be sure to provide them with this information. Of special interest will be any recent medication changes, episodes of depression, hospital stays, or other changes in routine.

If the physician and health care team are able to eliminate all reversible causes of his confusion and suggest that he is suffering from memory problems that will progress, you will need to take action. It is important for you and any other family members involved in your parent's care to begin to put together a flexible care plan, one that can easily be adjusted as his health and activity patterns change.

THE WORLD THROUGH YOUR PARENT'S EYES

If Dad suffers from confusion, planning a daily activity schedule is difficult, but not impossible. As dementia progresses, he will live mostly in the present, have little memory of the past, and be unable to anticipate the future. Since activities will not be anticipated or remembered, you will need to keep your parent happy and busy *for the moment.*

To him, the world looks like a giant and complicated jigsaw puzzle. Tasks that used to be accomplished easily, like putting on and tying shoes or going to the bathroom, now pose a major challenge. He forgets that he just ate and when he last bathed, and is sometimes confused about who different family members are. This can be frustrating, but there are some simple things you can do to make daily activities easier to get through for both of you. Practice seeing the world through his eyes—then try some new approaches for meeting his daily needs.

APPROACHES THAT WORK WITH CONFUSED PEOPLE

Dad's life is not over because he is confused, but he will need more help from you to remain happy and active. Here are some ideas to keep in mind as you and your parent move through the day.

√ *Directions should be simple and to the point. They should be given one step at a time.*
   Avoid saying things like, "Hurry up and get ready. We have to go to the store." Rather, try saying, "Come with

me." Offer only the information he really needs, and you will find he will seldom ask for more.

√ *Ask questions that can be answered with yes or no.*
Instead of saying, "Tell me all about your day," ask, "Did you have a good day?" Your parent may not be able to retrieve words needed for a full-sentence response, but the ability to respond to a simple yes or no question allows him to share in the joy of conversation.

√ *Limit choices to areas he can really understand or areas where making a wrong choice will not cause unnecessary problems.*
Your parent should not be given a choice whether to see the doctor about a cough, but he can be a full participant in choosing what he wants to eat at the dinner table.

√ *Remove any background noises before trying to communicate with your confused parent.*
Playing the radio or TV while you are giving instructions about dressing or some other task only increases the chance that he will not understand what you are saying to him. Use radio and TV only when those are the main activities the two of you are doing.

√ *Leave negatives out of sentences.*
Inappropriate behaviors should be gently but firmly redirected. Avoid saying, "Don't do that" or "no." Instead, say "Let's go over here together." Better yet, think ahead to minimize chances of getting into a situation in which inappropriate behavior is likely to occur. For instance, get your parent to the bathroom on a regular schedule to avoid accidents or urinating in inappropriate places. Protect him from agitating situations or events that might cause him to be combative.

√ *Consider overlooking some of his inappropriate behaviors to save him embarrassment and preserve his dignity.*
It is not necessary to move your parent if he accidentally sits in your seat at dinner. Instead, allow him to sit there, and you sit somewhere else for that meal.

√ *Validate his feelings when he says things that are not based in reality.*
Your mother has been gone for several years, but your father suddenly asks about her. Instead of reminding him that she died five years ago, reassure him that she is okay, and then go on to reminisce together about her. What he is really looking for are the warm, reassuring words and feelings he associates with your mother.

√ *Read body language.*
Forcing Dad to sit down when he appears to need to move around only makes him agitated. Assume that his body language (i.e. walking, pacing, or other anxious behavior) is a sign that he needs something. For instance, he could be cold, hungry, or have to go to the bathroom.

√ *Recognize that he may will substitute a word that comes to his mind for the word he really wants.*
For instance, he may call you his mother instead of his daughter, or he may use "him" to describe you instead of "her." Rather than correct him, give lots of love and reassurance that you are a person who truly cares about him. Your smile and touch tell him that you and he have a special relationship, even though he may not be able to totally sort out what the relationship is anymore.

As you work with your parent, you will quickly learn other ways to help him through the day.

CHANGES IN ACTIVITY PATTERNS

Dad has always been busy. He worked long hours, and filled his free time with bowling and fishing. Now that he cannot work anymore, he has a lot of time on his hands but little meaningful activity with which to fill it. This increases his anxiety level, and may cause him to pace or rearrange such items as furniture or paperwork that you would rather he not have rearranged.

It may be difficult for him to sit for more than a few minutes at a time. Forcing him to sit often makes his desire to move around even stronger. Allowing him the freedom to be up and about gives him a sense of control and reduces his anxiety.

You may find that as confusion increases, sleep patterns are interrupted. He used to sleep from 10:00 until 6:00—now, on a good night, he sleeps from 11:00 until 4:00. Planning lots of repetitive, active things to do during the day such as mall walks, sweeping the patio, help to prepare him for the best possible night's sleep.

ADJUSTING THE ENVIRONMENT

For your parent to be as active as possible without endangering himself or misplacing important items, it may be necessary to make some changes in the home environment. Items that he used safely in the past may now be inappropriate for him. Simplify his environment for maximum safety and activity.

- Lock drawers that hold important papers, knives, scissors, and other items that he might lose or use in an unsafe manner. This saves you from having to look for things you need and prevents him from injuring himself.

- Leave out some unimportant paper and writing materials for him to use and go through. If he loses them, it will not matter, and he may actually feel like he's back at work, opening mail and writing memos. Official-looking mail advertisements may work well for this purpose.

- Be aware of food or other items that could be put in the mouth and cause choking, poisoning, or other illness. For instance, if your parent is shelling peanuts, take precautions so that he does not eat the shells.

- Remove unnecessary furniture and knickknacks from the usual living areas. Leave a favorite chair, couch, or footstool, but be sure there is a clear path to each piece of furniture in order to prevent falls. Instead of glass bells or pewter bowls that might break or get lost, leave unbreakable items that can be of use in reminiscing—a model of an old car, a scrapbook of reminders of favorite pastimes, an Afghan made by your mother. Provide color contrast between furniture and floor—as your parent's dementia progresses, it will be harder for him to see where the floor ends and the chairs begin, making sitting down safely more difficult.

- Leave only three or four outfits in the closet and two or three pair of underwear and socks in his drawers. Fewer choices of what to wear will be less confusing to him, but still leave some clothes for him to be in control of and rummage through daily. In mid to late stages, where layering of clothing can be a problem, you may want to limit available clothing to one set and leave nonwearable items, such as handkerchiefs, washcloths, and towels, for rummaging, folding, and fondling.

- Keep a set of "traveling items" in a place where only you can access them. You may find that he hides things where neither of you can find them. Putting shoes, hat, jacket, and other necessary items away saves you time and frustration when you are ready to leave for that important appointment.

- A fenced yard, front and back, provides security, whether your parent still lives alone, or has moved in with you. The more room he has to walk and explore in a safe yard, the less likely he may be to wander. In later stages of dementia, wandering may become a real problem. Whether he has a caregiver in his home or lives with you, a door lock, placed high above his head, or a disguised lock should help to keep him safely in the house until you are ready to leave with him.

THINGS TO DO

√ Contact the Alzheimer's Association in your area and ask them to send you their basic information packet. Also, specifically request the booklet, "Steps to Selecting Activities for the Person with Alzheimer's Disease."

Note: Your older relative may be suffering from another dementing illness, such as multi-infarct dementia. The Alzheimer's Association can still be of assistance to you. While multi-infarct dementia and Alzheimer's disease have different points of origin in the body system, the end results of the dementia often look very similar.

√ Consider joining an Alzheimer's Association caregiver support group. Besides fellowship with other caregivers, some meetings also offer education and social functions. Visit the one closest to you this week.

√ Use a section of your spiral notebook to make notes on your parent's activity patterns. How much does he sleep? What makes him anxious? Does he sit in front of the TV and sleep most of the day, or does he spend the majority of his time pacing? How much of his own hygiene can he still do himself? Answering these and other questions will help you know where and how much to intervene.

√ Contact an area home health care agency or senior service agency to find out about cost and availability of home care workers or respite companions specially trained in the care of the cognitively impaired. Look in the Yellow Pages under Senior Citizens' Services or Home Health Services to find in-home help. Your Area Agency on Aging may also be able to send you a list of in-home services. Getting someone besides you involved in your parent's care now may help to avert a caregiving crisis later.

√ Read *The 36 Hour Day* by Mace and Rabins *or Understanding Alzheimer's Disease* by Howard Greutzner for a more complete look at progressive confusion and memory problems.

Chapter Six

ACTIVITIES WITH CONFUSED PARENTS

· · · · · · · · ·

"Dad's been so uncooperative lately. He won't get dressed in the morning, and his room is a mess. Nothing I serve for dinner seems to make him happy, and he won't get himself a snack from the frig when he's hungry. Baseball was always his favorite game—he watched it for hours. Now he doesn't enjoy TV at all. It sure makes it difficult to get through the day."

—*Marsha, age 51, teacher*

TO PLAN A SUCCESSFUL DAY WITH YOUR PARENT, UNDERSTAND and accept that he cannot change the way he behaves. Because of brain changes, he is no longer capable of learning significant new information and has a hard time just understanding the familiar. He relies heavily on you to provide verbal and environmental cues to help him through his increasingly confusing daily activities. Simplifying his environment and adjusting your expectations of him, will help both of you move through the day more smoothly.

A number of problems may contribute to his inability to get safely and happily through the day. They include:
- a short attention span
- inability to perform tasks with more than one step

- anxiety caused by the awareness of "losing thoughts"
- frequent mood swings
- poor judgment
- inability to read or inability to understand and process information he has read
- loss of awareness of time and place (not knowing the time, date, season, or where he is)
- confusion over what is real and what is not
- decreased ability to make desired body movements

Because of these limitations, the day will go a lot better for both of you if it is structured, yet easily adjustable to accommodate a mood change or an unexpected problem.

Use your spiral notebook to divide the day's activities into the categories explained in Chapter One. Start by identifying those things that *have to be done* and *should be done*. Considering your parent's confusion level, figure out approximately how much time it will take to accomplish these activities. Any time left over after his basic needs are met can be spent at a senior center (appropriate during the early stages of confusion), adult day program, running errands with you or another caregiver, or enjoying other special activities.

When you finish this chapter, you will have a better idea as to how you can plan the best day possible with your confused parent. There are hints on helping Dad in the bathroom, how to cue him so he can continue to care for many of his own hygiene needs, and what kinds of special activities many confused people enjoy most.

GETTING DOWN TO BASICS

Everyday things Dad used to do by himself without a thought are now difficult or impossible. Using some simple techniques to aid him in completing these tasks builds his self-esteem, and makes your day easier, too.

TOILETING

Allow your parent to do toileting-related tasks as long as he can. Once he begins having problems, help him only as much as absolutely necessary (for instance, he may need you to tell him where he can find the bathroom, but manage fine once he finds it). As he becomes more dependent in toileting, use these suggestions to help him remain continent as long as possible:

- Label the bathroom door "toilet," "bathroom," or whatever term is most meaningful to Dad.
- Ask him if he needs to use the bathroom, or take him to the bathroom on a regular schedule, say every two to three hours.
- Provide contrasting colors for the floor and toilet seat so that your parent can clearly see where to sit.
- Install handrails for ease of getting on and off the toilet.
- Place a sign above the toilet paper roll to identify it, if necessary.

In mid to late stages of progressive dementia, someone will need to walk Dad through each step of the bathroom process:

- Help him to the bathroom.
- Open the door for him, or ask him to open the door.
- Assist him in removing his lower body clothing.
- Aid him verbally and physically in sitting down.
- Help him find and tear the toilet paper to wipe, or actually wipe him.
- Assist him in redressing.
- Remind him to flush, or flush for him.
- Lead him to the sink and remind him to wash his hands.

Eventually your parent will probably need to wear some kind of undergarment adult protection. Make this fact a part of your adjustable care-activity plan early on. It is important to accept that at some point the use of adult pads, along with regular trips to the bathroom, may be the most dignified and reasonable way to help your parent handle bathroom-related tasks.

SLEEP

The best way to ensure a good night's sleep for your confused parent (and for you!) is to engage him in plenty of physical exercise during the day. Give repetitive tasks to do, such as sweeping the patio or polishing the car. (Be careful in later stages of confusion that he does not attempt to eat the polish.) Provide Dad with opportunities for walking. Here are some additional ideas for getting your parent to bed and asleep:

- Establish a consistent evening routine—one that he can count on.
- Be available at bedtime. Relieve any fears he may have regarding the security of the house—let him walk around to check locks with you or, if possible, let him lead in this activity. Reassure him about any other areas of concern.
- Provide him the opportunity to use the bathroom and have a *small* drink of water before bed.
- Inform him that you are preparing for bed also.

While some people with progressive confusion and memory loss sleep well, others get their days and nights mixed up. If you are not able to sleep at least six hours a night using the above suggestions, a request from your parent's physician for medication to aid in the sleep process may partially solve the problem. Always monitor the effects of medications carefully if you have to use them. Because of potential side effects, they should be used only in extreme situations where nothing else works.

HYGIENE

Bathing, brushing teeth, and other grooming and hygiene activities are often forgotten in the early stages of confusion, or cannot be initiated independently. Dad may not remember to bathe, may think he has just bathed, and may actually have some fears about being in water. Some ways to help him accomplish these hygiene tasks include:

Bathing

◊ *Keep a sense of humor about bathing.* With your arm around him, say something like, "We've got a hot date with Betty Grable tonight. Let's get ready!" Yes, this is a slight untruth, but it is light and fun, and uses a familiar name to which your parent can relate. He will not remember later what name you used, but he will retain a general feeling of calm and well-being because you used a fun approach to help get him washed.

◊ *Recognize that he may not need to bathe or shower every day.* He grew up when a bath once a week was okay. He also does not sweat as much as he did when he was younger.

◊ *Substitute a sponge bath for a regular bath or shower when possible.* Your parent can probably assist with his sponge bath for a long time, and it may be less threatening to him than a full bath or shower.

◊ *Respect his right to privacy.* Older adults grew up in a day when people were more modest about their bodies. Even in late stages of dementia, when you think Dad is no longer aware, a towel or robe can be worn into the shower and removed at the last minute to ensure dignity.

Teeth, Shaving, and Hair Care

◊ *Label all necessary items as he becomes more confused.* Items you might want to label include toothbrush, cup, razor (electric or safety), and hairbrush or comb.

◊ *Put needed hygiene items out one at a time.* For instance, accomplish tooth brushing and put these items away; then get out the shaving equipment, and so on. As confusion progresses, you will need to put the toothpaste on the brush, put the brush in his hand, and say, "Brush your teeth." The simpler the environment, the less trouble your parent will have getting through his necessary daily activities.

◊ *Expect less than perfection.* In later stages of confusion and memory loss, you may want to "touch up" Dad's shaving job. Do so in earlier stages only with his permission and with a good sense of humor.

Eating

Simplifying the eating environment will extend his independence. Try these ideas the next time the two of you sit down to eat:

◊ Provide him with only the utensils he needs to eat the meal you are serving.

◊ Put only one or two different foods on the plate at a time.

◊ Offer small amounts of food the first time around. This will be less confusing than piling a lot of food on his plate. Give him seconds as he desires.

◊ Cue your parent to begin eating in later stages of confusion by putting his spoon in his hand. He may then be able to continue feeding himself.

◊ Using fingers eliminates the need for utensils, so serve finger foods as he becomes more confused. Remember that the more items in and around his eating area, the more confused he may become.

SPECIAL ACTIVITIES TO ENJOY

Whether he attends church with you, walks in the park with his home health aide, or takes a trip to the zoo with friends from his adult day program, your parent needs to experience special activities designed to stimulate him physically, spiritually, cognitively, socially, and emotionally. Some activity ideas that keep many confused people happily occupied follow.

Music

Tuning in radio stations that play all the great tunes from the 1920s to the 1950s helps your parent relive "dancing cheek to cheek." Remember that conflicting background noises, such as people talking and having the radio and TV on simultaneously, may work for you, but definitely not for your confused loved one. Music benefits him most if he does not have to try to distinguish it from competing sounds in his environment.

Watch his reaction to music. Does he sing along? Do his feet tap to the beat? Give Dad opportunities to enjoy the music that has been part of his life. Was he a country fan? Did he sing in a church choir? If he enjoyed classical music, plan a night out to listen to a chamber orchestra or the symphony.

If he has problems recalling the words he wants to say, try letting him talk through music. He will often be able to remember words to music even when he cannot find the words he needs for normal conversation. Singing the old tunes allows your parent pleasant memories, as well as supports his need to use language.

Music that is too loud or has a very intense beat is agitating for confused people. Keep looking for the rhythm, the kind of music, and the music era that keeps the twinkle in your parent's eyes.

Dancing

Dancing provides the best of music and exercise. Use a quiet moment at home to dance around the family room with your parent. This can be a moment shared by the two of you, or include any other family members or friends who are willing to give it a try.

At the local senior center, spend a night dancing to some of your parent's favorite music from the past. Even if he does not remember the dance the next day, he will be happy while there. If Dad attends an adult day program, arrange for him to be there on dance days. (Many participants at our adult day program say they have either never danced or have not danced in years, but once they are persuaded to give it a try, they love it.)

Because of the disease process in his brain, your parent may not glide around the floor the way he used to, so do not expect Arthur Murray (of course, he may surprise you!). Just moving to the rhythm of the music is enough.

Walking

Walking is great exercise for confused elders, and often is a substitute for other meaningful activities that can no longer be enjoyed. Both the desire and the ability to walk remain with many older people, even those suffering from advanced confusion. Here are some suggestions for making walking a more enjoyable activity:

- Falling is less likely in flat shoes, so purchase a supportive pair of walking shoes.
- Provide your parent with an identification bracelet, and include a card with his address and phone number in his wallet.
- Have him take walks in a shopping mall, or outside if the weather is nice.
- If he does not have a problem getting lost, encourage him to walk by himself to close, familiar places.
- Walk Dad if he seems confused about where he is going, or if he begins to lose his way in familiar territory.
- Seek out an adult day program that provides daily supervised walks.

Working

Your parent has not forgotten about work just because he no longer holds down a job. Older adults who attend day programs or are in nursing homes often believe they are at work. The right kind of work brings a sense of accomplishment and fulfillment in spite of confusion. Supply jobs that involve repetition and no new steps—tasks that will allow success and enhancement of his sense of accomplishment and self-worth.

- Offer paperwork projects such as making "to do" lists, writing letters, and clipping coupons from the newspaper.
- Keep a broom handy for sweeping dirt and leaves off the patio or walk.
- Have a basket of tea towels and underwear handy, ready to be folded and refolded.
- Provide peas or peanuts to shell, or beans to snap.
- Make other esteem-building tasks available, such as winding yarn, sanding wood, and washing dishes.

Cooking and Eating

Sensory stimulation refers to the fact that several, if not all, of Dad's senses are involved in interpreting and enjoying an activity. One activity that involves many senses is cooking. People with Alzheimer's disease and other progressive dementias enjoy simple cooking projects but often cannot accomplish the many steps involved without some guidance. Here is how you might structure a cooking activity for your confused parent:

- Set aside an hour to accomplish some other kitchen task while you are assisting with the cake.
- Give one instruction at a time (for instance, "Pour the cake mix into the bowl. Now fill the measuring cup up to this mark with water. Now pour the water in the bowl").
- Ask your parent to beat the cake mix and then allow as much time as needed to accomplish this task.

- Offer to finish the job if it becomes frustrating. It is not as important that the task be finished as that it be enjoyed.

Cooking is a great sensory activity because it looks, smells, and tastes good; it also offers stimulation through the sense of touch. One of the most popular activities in our day program is cooking, and then eating what we have created. Having the elder create something that can be enjoyed right away is a pleasant way of rewarding confused elders for a job well done.

A word of caution: Be sure to closely monitor kitchen activities. Smoke and fire caused by food left on the stove too long, or burns caused from a spilled pot of boiling water can be prevented if you keep a watchful eye on all food preparation and cooking activities.

Creative Activities (Arts and Crafts)

Not all elders enjoy arts and crafts, but many find pleasure in creating. Even if creative arts have not been part of your parent's background, you might try some simple art projects. Here are some ideas that may work for you and your confused parent.

- *Water Color Painting.* This is an art medium that assures success. No matter how simple or elaborate, a water color painting is an expression of the self.
- *Collage Creation.* Collages express any theme, from people to animals, to beautiful scenery. Even if your parent cannot use scissors anymore, he can search magazine pages for pictures and help attach them to construction paper or poster board.
- *Nail Art.* Pound large nails into a block of wood. Have your parent wrap yarn around the nails in different colors and patterns. The yarn can be undone at a later date and the block and nails reused.

- *Clay Design.* Clay can be molded or imprinted with designs. Anything can be used to imprint the clay: a plastic knife, coin, and cookie cutters, for example. Depending on how far you and your parent wish to take the project, the clay can even be baked to preserve the mold or design permanently.
- *Flower Gathering and Pressing.* Gathering and pressing flowers can bring great pleasure and enjoyment to many older people. Your parent cannot make a mistake doing it—it is an activity that is always successful, no matter what flowers you pick or how they look after they are pressed.

There are many other creative projects to do with your confused parent. Adapt other simple ideas from craft books to meet your particular needs.

THINGS TO DO

√ Visit a senior center in your area to observe the functioning level of center visitors. Plan to have lunch there in order to really assess how well your parent would fit in.

√ Consult any publications aimed at the senior market for information on recreation discounts for seniors in your area. You can find senior publications listed in the Yellow Pages under "Newspapers." Then figure out which restaurants and places of entertainment would be most appropriate for your parent to attend with you.

√ Start a collection of tapes/records/CDs of songs from the Twenties through the Fifties. If your parent has been religious, some music related to church or synagogue would also be nice to have on hand.

√ Begin a list of quick mix/no bake recipes. Because confused elders often lose a lot of weight, enjoying food is not just a pleasant activity, but a necessary one.

√ Arrange a night out for a ball game or a meal at your parent's favorite eatery. It is important for both of you to continue to enjoy these special activities for as long as possible.

√ Order the *Anderson Planner* from Rosewood Publishing, Star Route Box 145, Sarona, WI 54870. This inexpensive planner ($28 per year) is full of ideas for word games, crafts, and special holiday celebrations. While not all ideas in the planner will work with confused elders, many can be adapted to meet their needs.

√ Read *Failure-Free Activities for the Alzheimer's Patient*, by Carmel Sheridan, and *Doing Things*, by Zola Jitka. If the books are not available at your local public library, try interlibrary loan, or order them through your favorite bookstore.

√ Check out the Lubidet (Loobiday) or a comparable product for a warm water wash and warm air dry after using the bathroom. For someone who has lost the ability to wipe themselves, this could work well.

√ Contact the Alzheimer's Association nearest you for information on "Project Safe Return," a network for finding people with memory loss or confusion who have wandered away.

Chapter Seven

STAYING BUSY WITH PHYSICAL AND SENSORY LOSSES

. . . .

"When Mom's eyesight began to fail, she got very depressed. She couldn't see to read or crochet anymore. She's always had a little arthritis, but lately it's gotten so much worse. Now she even has trouble getting her clothes on and off. I can only imagine how Mom must feel, losing her eyesight and suffering with arthritis all at the same time."

—*Jeff, real estate agent, age 52*

MANY CAREGIVERS TAKE PRIDE IN THEIR PARENT'S ABILITY TO care for themselves. Independence is possible as long as Mom stays healthy; but when health-related losses begin, you may have questions as to whether she is still able to make it on her own.

When your parent experiences physical and sensory losses that limit her ability to interact effectively with her world, you are faced with a dilemma. How soon should you intervene? Can she still survive on her own? Will she be angry if you suggest that she move out of her home and in with you, or into assisted living?

While physical and sensory losses may limit Mom's activity, adaptations can be made that may enable her to continue to partially care for herself. Simple changes in her environment, as well as the utilization of some special resources and approaches, help her continue to function in an independent setting.

This chapter begins by reviewing some of the most common physical and sensory problems of aging. It then gives information on approaches and resources that support activity in spite of losses. Finally, activities are suggested that allow aging parents with physical and sensory losses to continue to feel fulfilled, productive, and happy.

COMMON PHYSICAL LOSSES OF AGING

Physical problems of aging can limit Mom's desire and ability to join in a special activity or to perform daily self-care tasks. Let's look at how physical losses may discourage your parent's continued involvement in active living. Several common disease processes that may affect your loved one as she gets older include stroke, heart disease, diabetes, arthritis, and Parkinson's disease. Consult a medical dictionary, library books, or your physician for a complete and professional definition of these diseases. Also consult a physician specialist for a complete examination as necessary.

Mobility and Dexterity Issues

Each of the disease processes listed above may in some way affect your parent's ability to be mobile. Suffering a stroke, for instance, often makes it difficult, and sometimes impossible, to move the arm and leg on the affected side of the body. Parkinson's disease causes the limbs to "turn off" in terms of their ability to move. Arthritis can totally disable, or it can limit mobility with painful reminders each time your parent tries to use an arm or leg.

In some cases, medication, exercise, and rest can assist your parent in regaining dexterity and mobility. She may find that after she has taken her Parkinson's medication, her limbs "turn on," enabling her to complete some tasks. Prescribed exercise and physical therapy can improve your parent's post-stroke recovery, allowing her to regain movement on the affected side.

Weakness

Stroke, Parkinson's, arthritis, and other diseases of aging can cause weakness. Joints, muscles, and bones deteriorate from lack of use and from disease processes, making it difficult to stay active.

Depression often further limits the ability to accomplish daily tasks. The generalized feeling of weakness that can result from these diseases, and accompanying depression, are often more debilitating than the disease processes themselves.

Mom may allow the presence of weakness or pain to inhibit the use of affected limbs or other body parts. More weakness then results, followed by another decrease in movement. Given this kind of cycle, your parent could become bedbound very quickly. She has learned a helplessness that, without intervention, will perpetuate itself. Some activities and changes in her environment that may help break this cycle will be suggested later in this chapter.

Nutritional and Dietary Concerns

Lifetime nutrition and dietary habits contribute to one's present health. What your parent eats today continues to affect her health, especially if she has had a stroke or suffers from heart disease or diabetes.

While dietary issues are important for health, eating is an activity most older people can still enjoy, in spite of losses they may have suffered. An overly harsh or restrictive diet, unless absolutely necessary, may promote unhappiness and cause more harm than good.

When Cognitive Impairment Exists with Physical Loss

Some physical conditions, such as stroke and Parkinson's disease, can be accompanied by cognitive impairment that may cause your parent to make inappropriate judgments regarding physical capabilities.

It is important for you to be aware of cognitive deficiencies that may exist along with physical loss. Because of her cognitive challenges, Mom might think she is able to ambulate on her own, while physically, she really cannot do so. Being educated on issues of cognitive impairment puts you in a good position to support your parent if both physical and cognitive challenges are present. Start by talking to Mom's physician about possible problems of cognition associated with her physical illnesses.

SENSORY LOSSES OF AGING

Besides the obvious physical problems that are often present as your parent ages, many elders also experience moderate to severe sensory losses. While all five senses may be somewhat affected, loss of hearing, sight, and taste are probably the most difficult for your parent to overcome.

Hearing Loss

If your parent is losing her hearing, she is also losing an important communication tool. Because of her loss, you will both have to work harder at the communication necessary to successfully complete daily activities. Lowering the tone of your voice may help.

To better identify with what your hearing impaired parent is going through, try sitting at the far end of a table when out for lunch with a group. Experience the frustration of attempting to hear the conversation at the other end of the table, and how it feels to be left out.

Try this experiment the next time you get together with family and friends: Cover your ears with headphones and see how much of the surrounding conversation you are able to pick up. Because you will not be able to hear very well, you can practice figuring out what is being said by paying attention to body language and attempting to read lips.

Your parent may actually believe that people, including you, are talking softly because they are talking about her. This can lead to paranoia, increased communication problems, and decreased cooperation in the accomplishment of daily tasks and activities.

Eyesight Loss

Good eyesight provides an open door to continued interaction with the surrounding environment. As cataracts, glaucoma, and other eye diseases appear, your parent's ability to write checks, watch television, sew or knit, do crossword puzzles, or navigate safely through her living area decreases. Many eye problems can be corrected with surgery or glasses, but some do not respond to correction procedures, or such procedures are not recommended by a physician due to other health problems. Good contrast is needed, as well as large print books, cards, and games.

Because of eyesight loss, Mom's world is smaller, darker, and more frightening. She is at greater risk of falling, and will not be able to participate in many of the activities she previously enjoyed. Your understanding and support are important in helping her adjust to a less visual world.

Loss of Taste

As your parent ages, the sense of taste is less acute than it once was. This may cause her to oversalt food, or put too much sugar in her coffee.

Dieticians in care facilities and hospitals, whose job it is to see that healthy nutritional standards are maintained, often order bland diets for elderly patients or residents. In care facilities, dieticians and activities directors may have mild disagreements about what constitutes a quality food-related experience for residents. While it is important to be aware of nutrition, especially in situations where eating certain foods or using too much of a condiment could cause a health crisis, caregivers should attempt to strike a balance. Good nutritional practices go hand in hand with an awareness that eating is a pleasure your parent can still enjoy. Restricting it too much may contribute to depression and give her one less reason to live.

Sometimes caregivers think parents try to frustrate them by acting like they cannot hear, see, or taste very well. Although some elders may act this way, most do not do so. It is therefore important to take sensory deficits seriously. Do what you can to offer support, and assist her in making necessary lifestyle changes as comfortably as possible.

RESOURCES AND APPROACHES THAT LESSEN THE IMPACT OF LOSSES

Helping your parent handle physical challenges demands a balanced approach between accepting losses and working together to improve daily functioning in spite of them. Here are some ideas for building on strengths and assisting Mom or Dad in meeting each day's new challenge in the areas of physical and sensory loss.

- *Recognize the importance of movement.*
  Whether your parent's movement is in the form of swimming exercise at the Y while you work out, physical therapy following a stroke, or leg and arm lifts she does with her home health aide, it needs to happen on a regular basis to keep joints and muscles working flexibly. Check with Mom's physician to establish appropriate exercise limits.

- *Consider medical or even surgical intervention.*
  While surgery is not always indicated, procedures like cataract surgery are now done frequently and successfully.

Sometimes hearing can be improved simply by having wax removed from the ear canal. Your parent is probably no more fond of surgical/medical procedures than you are. Be sensitive to her wishes, but share your honest opinion if you feel the procedure will give her a better quality of life.

- *Alter her environment for safety and ease of mobility.*
  Handrails, solid furniture placed to provide support as Mom moves from room to room, and clear pathways for travel about the home or apartment help her continue to live independently. Eliminate throw rugs or other obstacles on the floor that might cause her to fall. Be sure kitchen and utility items used on a regular basis are within easy reach. To avoid accidental poisoning, dangerous items, such as bleach or other household cleaners, should be clearly labeled for sight-impaired parents. This labeling could be accomplished through raised lettering on the container that your parent could trace with her finger.

- *Provide night-lights to aid your parent in traveling through the house in the dark.*
  It is easy for your parent to forget exactly where she is in the dark, and to stumble and fall. Taking a wrong turn on the way to the kitchen could result in a fall down the stairs. Overstepping the toilet might cause her to trip and land in the bathtub. Providing adequate lighting makes disorientation and falls less likely.

- *Purchase adaptive clothing, as it become necessary, so she can continue to dress herself.*
  Be slow to change the way your parent has always dressed. Freedom to choose her clothing is an important sign of independence. If, however, she has suffered a stroke or has arthritis or Parkinson's disease, adaptive clothing may be appropriate to enable her to continue to dress herself.

Clothing that is easy to get up and down may also help keep her independent in bathroom-related tasks. Sweat suits; Velcro instead of buttons or ties; and loose housedresses without buttons, ties, or snaps work well for many physically challenged people.

- *Offer touching and feeling experiences to elders with physical and sensory losses.*
  Mom may feel her physical and sensory losses less if you offer increased physical interaction in terms of hugs, kisses, or perhaps just a supportive arm. Your touch may fill a large part of the void she feels because of her losses, and may also build on the ability and desire she has to show warmth and love.

- *Select appropriate medical equipment as needed to support the elder's independence.*
  While your parent may say she will never use a walker, wheelchair, or other assistive device, the time could come when her safety and independence depend on her using one. Adaptive bowls, silverware, and cups are also available to aid in independent eating for elders with physical challenges, such as stroke or Parkinson's disease. A raised toilet seat and grip bars on the walls may greatly increase her ability to be independent in the bathroom. Such devices can be obtained from hospitals or medical supply houses near you. Consult the Yellow Pages for supply houses in your area.

- *Arrange for people to look in on your parent at regular intervals.*
  It is tough to try to be your parent's only caregiver. It makes a lot of sense to enlist friends, neighbors, church acquaintances, or other volunteers to help you care for her early in the caregiving process.

- *Offer the opportunity to achieve completion of segments of tasks rather than full tasks.* Your parent may not have the strength or perseverance to complete a task from beginning to end. Segmenting the task into small pieces, and encouraging completion of just a portion of it builds self-esteem and confidence.

With these and other supports, Mom may be able to maintain her independence and care for herself. The satisfaction she feels from successfully and independently handling many of her daily living tasks may encourage her to participate in fun activities she might not have chosen otherwise.

Remember that the first chapter of this book suggested three different areas in which your parent needs to stay active. They were:

- Things that *have to be done*, like sleeping, going to the bathroom, and eating.
- Things that *should be done*, such as bathing, brushing teeth, and grooming.
- Things that your parent *likes and chooses to do*, such as attending movies and listening to music.

So far in this chapter we have discussed assisting your parent with physical and sensory impairment through daily activities that have to be, and should be, done. Now let us discuss some activities that your parent likes, or chooses to do, and find out how they can be enjoyed in spite of physical and sensory challenges.

SPECIAL ACTIVITIES FOR ELDERS WITH PHYSICAL AND SENSORY IMPAIRMENTS

You may hear complaints from your parent that she cannot do much of anything since her eyesight got so bad and she broke her hip. While it is true that everything may take more effort than it used to, she can still enjoy many special activities. Here are a few that you may want to try.

Movement to Music

Visually impaired elders, as well as those with stroke, Parkinson's disease, heart disease, and other medical problems, can benefit from movement to music. Besides the exercise, there is value in being touched and held while moving to the beat of the music.

If your parent is hearing impaired, be sure she is as close to the music as possible. For a parent who has suffered a stroke, carefully support her so she does not fall. It is not necessary that she actually move around the dance floor to enjoy the activity. Just swaying from side to side, or moving her arms while you move your feet, provides exercise, touching, and pleasure.

Listening Activities

If Mom cannot read the paper anymore because of vision impairment, she may still interact with reading materials through books on tape. The Library for the Blind makes tape recorders and tapes available, free of charge, on a variety of subjects. Most public libraries also have a wide selection of books on tape, including classics, present-day dramatic and adventure stories, and self-help topics.

While radio stations today play a different kind of music than your parent listened to when she was young, some carry special musical presentations or talk shows that are more appropriate for older listeners. Our day program participants here in Denver, for instance, enjoy listening to a local radio station that features Big Band hits from the Thirties and Forties.

Conversational Activities

It is important for your parent to continue to converse and socialize in spite of physical and sensory challenges. A parent with impaired speech due to a stroke still needs to talk, even if it is only through body language. If hearing loss is present, there is still benefit in communicating in tones she can hear, or through written messages.

Taking the time to make eye contact with Mom, or, if she is sight-impaired, to gently touch her hand while you talk with her sends a message that you really do care. Whatever was actually shared conversationally takes on added meaning because you took the time to show that you were actively listening.

Hands-on Projects

Cutting out coupons, working with paint or clay, sanding wood, and cooking are all hands-on activities that can be done by many people with physical and sensory impairments. If Dad can only use one hand, let him sand while you steady the wood. Mom's sight may be impaired, but she can still participate in a cooking project because she can feel the spoon and the bowl.

An elderly parent with heart disease or diabetes may feel too weak to dance, but may be able to paint, cut out coupons, or do clay sculptures easily from a sitting position. Rolling balls of yarn and folding clothes may be enough stimulation for some elders with physical and sensory losses, while others will be able to play the piano or tap to the beat.

Food-related Activities

Your parent may have poor eyesight and limited ability to walk, but good food still brings her a lot of pleasure. She will enjoy food-related activities, whether it be a quiet meal at home with you or dining out at a favorite restaurant.

The aroma of foods, as well as unique food tastes, help stimulate the senses. Have a tasting party, trying different cheeses, various kinds of popcorn, or unique flavors of ice cream.

Games

Tossing a ball or balloon around the family room is fun, and provides a means of exercise. An indoor putter allows your parent to swing a golf club even when it is cold outside, and a laundry basket or wastebasket makes a good hoop for indoor basketball.

Word games and other guessing games provide an opportunity for intellectual challenge. They can be adapted to meet the needs of just about anyone with physical or sensory impairment.

THINGS TO DO

√ Check out books that discuss diseases or problems experienced by your parent. Start early so you can stay a step ahead of issues that may surface as disease symptoms progress.

√ Try eating a meal without seasoning your food. You will not get a perfect picture of how your parent's food tastes, but the experience will help you relate better to your parent's diminished sense of taste.

√ In the Yellow Pages, check for names of companies that make and supply adaptive clothing, or contact an activities director from a local care facility. Here are a couple of places to contact: Adaptogs, Inc., Rt. 1, Box 76, Otis, CO 80743, (303) 246-3761; M & M Health Care Apparel Co., 1541 60th Street, Brooklyn, NY 12129. Think about what kind of clothing could be adopted from your favorite department store to meet your parent's needs.

√ Order some resources that will help you identify word games and active games that are appropriate for your parent. Here are the names, addresses, and phone numbers of two companies that specialize in activity ideas for individuals who have physical and sensory challenges: Creative Resources, PO Box 328, Etowah, NC 28729, (704) 891-2919; Hammatt Senior Products, PO Box 727, Mount Vernon, WA 98273, (206) 428-5850.

√ Visit a medical supply store to familiarize yourself with available resources that may be of help to your parent. You may also want to try these mail order businesses: MaxiAids, PO Box 3209, Farmingdale, NY 11735, (516) 752-0521; J. A. Preston Corp., PO Box 89, Jackson, MI 48204, (800) 631-7277.

√ Some of the best mental stimulation activities may come from your own creative thinking. Following are some ideas for games I have created and used successfully:

◊   *What do you buy at a:*
    Hardware store?
    Dime store?
    Grocery store?
    Department store?

◊   *Game of the states (sample questions):*
    What state is known for growing potatoes?
    Which states were part of the gold rush?
    What state is known for its earthquakes?

◊   *Names of things and people from the past:*
    cars
    cigarettes
    movie stars
    singers

It does not take long to pull ideas for both mental stimulation and active games from your own experience and adapt them to meet your parent's present situation.

Chapter Eight

WHEN THE TIME COMES FOR OUTSIDE HELP

· · · · · · · · ·

"Dad has lived with me for about three years now. It's tough keeping up with everything that needs to be done. I'm not sure how much longer I can manage both of our lives without some support. I wish there was somewhere I could go to get dependable, quality help with Dad."

—*Jeanne, florist, age 56*

IF YOUR PARENT'S CARE BECOMES INCREASINGLY DIFFICULT, keeping him active can be a full-time job. Between the support he needs each day to do all the things he has to do and should do, and arranging special activities, it is hard to find time to address important issues of your own.

You may be aware that you are nearing the end of your solo caregiving role, but do not know where to look for help. As you begin to search for assistance, you will find that there is an increasing number of care support options available.

This chapter helps you think creatively about long-term care opportunities that will support quality of life, while relieving you of some of the pressures associated with caring for your loved one. Extended family care, day programs, in-home care, board and care, retirement centers, assisted living centers, and nursing homes all exist for this reason.

When you finish this chapter, you should be familiar with a variety of long-term care services, and know how they may contribute to a continued active and productive life for your parent. You will also know how to find them, and be able to make a decision about which service or package of services will work best for both of you.

HOME AND COMMUNITY BASED CARE SYSTEMS

A number of transitional living options are available to help your parent maintain some independence in active living for as long as possible. They include extended family care, day programs, in-home care services, and board and care settings. Sometimes a combination of these services can be used to provide the best care situation.

Extended Family Care

From time to time, other family members or close friends may have offered help. Take them up on their offer.

Find some time to educate family or friends on techniques of care that have worked best for you. How do you accomplish a shower successfully? What special activities does your parent look forward to? Have you and Dad worked out special approaches to handle eating problems?

Successful caregiving is an art, accomplished by implementing techniques we have covered in this book. Relatives or friends who help to keep the elder active will appreciate knowing what you have learned about the art of caregiving before they become direct caregivers.

A short rest from caregiving may make it possible for you to provide care at home longer. We have participants in our day program who spend three or four months with a family member in Denver, and then travel to be with a son or daughter in another state. This allows part of the family to rest, while another family member temporarily picks up the major caregiving responsibility.

Sometimes people who offer support disagree on how much care an elder needs. They may not accept the presence of dementia, or be willing to admit that a stroke condition is not going to improve. Because they minimize the presence of a problem, it is difficult for them to support the caregiving venture.

Often, a family conference with a professional caregiver helps everyone see the need for care and activity support. If family and friends are still in denial and you cannot get their support, try calling on acquaintances from church, and civic and community organizations, to fill in so you can get an occasional break.

Day Programs

Since the 1970s, day programs have aided caregivers in avoiding premature nursing home placement for their loved one. Many times, elders are placed in care facilities, not so much because they need to be there, but because caregivers are burned out.

Besides helping caregivers avoid burnout, day programs are unique in their ability to provide an appropriate experience for all who attend. Some participants may see it as going to school or work, while others may enjoy the intellectual challenge of word games or discussions of current events.

Day programs offer activities that keep participants as busy as they wish to be, from the time they arrive until they go home at the end of the day. Because your parent has been active all day, he may get a better night's sleep, allowing you to sleep well also.

Your parent benefits from a variety of experiences and services at the day program. He socializes and makes new friends, staying stimulated through group discussions; keeps physically fit through daily exercise; participates in creative activities such as arts and crafts, dance, and music; and is monitored for physical and nutritional problems. Day programs provide lunch, with snacks as needed or desired throughout the day. Some programs also serve breakfast.

You may find a day program in your area that is offering more than daily care from 8:00 A.M. to 5:00 P.M. Day programs around the United States are attempting to give caregivers services they need and want by offering weekend day services; short-term overnight care; baths and shampoos; and other services, such as toenail care, escorts to the doctor's office, physical and occupational therapy, and speech services either at or through the program.

While your parent may not like the idea of being at the day program at first, most people grow to love it. Here are some hints for getting the person for whom you care to the day center the first few times (or until he finds out how much fun it can be!).

- *If your parent is cognitively intact, spend an hour or so discussing the center with him.*

  It can be difficult promoting activity and social involvement at home. Seniors like your parent, while they may tell you they want to stay at home, are often lonely and need a little encouragement from you to stay involved in the community outside the home. Tell your parent about the center and what happens there, and then ask him to give it a try for at least a month. If he attends that long, he should be hooked!

- *If your parent is minimally confused, tell him as little as possible about the center before a visit.*

  For a parent with confusion caused by Alzheimer's disease or some other dementia, it makes little sense to share a lot of details about the day program. It may make you feel like you are being more honest with your parent, but because of Dad's confusion, it only makes him anxious or agitated.

If the person for whom you care is in the very early stages of dementia, it is important to give him some basic information about where he will be visiting. Explain briefly that he will meet new friends and have a chance to pursue some favorite activities while he is there, and that you will be able to work and rest. Arguing about attendance will lead to failure. State positively that this is something you want to try that will be helpful to you both, and then redirect his attention to other things until the day of the visit.

• *If your parent has progressed to a stage of dementia that causes him to be argumentative or combative, or if he is so confused that he cannot make a correct judgment anymore, you should tell him as little as possible.*

Try saying something like, "We're going to visit some friends for lunch," or simply, "We're going for a ride in the car." If confusion is very advanced, just offer your hand and say, "Come with me." Once you have arrived at the center, let day program staff members help you make your parent comfortable. They will reassure your parent that you will be back to pick him up. Do not be overly concerned about his reaction to the next scheduled visit because much, if not all, of the first visit may be forgotten.

While considering using the day program, remember that while your parent may not want to attend in the beginning, he also may not like the idea of being moved to a more institutional living situation. "Sharing" his care with a day program may be the most acceptable choice for both of you as you find it necessary to withdraw from providing total care.

Most day programs are nonprofit, and costs for services vary between $25 and $35 per day. In some areas of the country, prices may be slightly higher or lower.

Payment for day program services can be private, through Medicaid (depending on the state), or, in some cases, through Title III funds or private insurance. Transportation to and from the program is usually available. Contact your Area Agency on Aging, or look under "day programs" or "senior services" in the Yellow Pages to find day programs in your area.

In-Home Care

Perhaps your parent truly is content being at home, watching TV and visiting with neighbors. Maybe your only problem caring for him is in assisting with his weekly bathing or housekeeping tasks.

In this case, a home health aide or personal care provider may be able to come in two to three times a week while you work, socialize a bit, help with baths, and tidy the living area. While home health is often available for 24-hour care, it is commonly used in 2- to 4-hour blocks at regular times each week.

Most areas of the country have numerous personal care and home health agencies. Depending on the level of care your parent needs, the agency will provide you with an appropriate caregiver. Services range from bathing and other personal care to full nursing services. Agencies generally charge $10 per hour and up. Some have scholarships or sliding fee scales.

Home health can also be used in conjunction with the day program so that activities of daily living can be accomplished at home, while more extensive socialization and special activities can be enjoyed at the day program. Home healthcare twice a week and attendance at a day program twice a week may be the best care combination, with you providing care the rest of the time.

Some day programs are now offering in-home care with staff specifically trained to meet the needs of the cognitively impaired population. Larger blocks of care are provided so that caregivers can get away for a short vacation or have a needed surgery. These home health and personal care workers approach care from the standpoint of making *all* daily activities come together in a quality-of-life experience for the cognitively impaired individual.

Home care, while sometimes covered by Medicare, Medicaid, or private insurance, can be quite costly if it is needed on a daily or 24-hour basis. Try to figure out exactly what care support you and your parent need, and whether home health should be part of your care picture. Find home health services in the Yellow Pages under "home health" or "personal care provider services," or through your Area Agency on Aging.

Residential-Based Care Systems

You may have promised Dad that you would never put him in a nursing home, but the time may come when some kind of residential care will be necessary in order to successfully carry out his daily activities.

There are many residential care options available today, from board and care or assisted living to nursing homes. The type of care you choose depends on your parent's functioning level, your financial resources, and, to some extent, the type of setting that appeals to you the most. If he has the cognitive ability to make appropriate decisions regarding his future living situation, your parent should also be an active participant in the decision-making process. Planning *early* is crucial. Research what is available with your parent before you have to make a residential placement decision.

Transitional Settings

Board and care, assisted living, and alternative care facilities are settings that provide a transitional step between a private home or apartment and a care facility. They are identified by a number of different names. In some states, assisted living and personal care boarding homes deliver the same services; assisted living centers may be licensed as personal care boarding homes.

You may also hear the term *alternative care facility*. In some states, the alternative care facility is a personal care boarding home that has been certified to accept Medicaid residents. Check with your Area Agency on Aging to find out what transitional living opportunities are available in your region, what they are called, and what services they offer.

If your parent is still able to do quite a number of things for himself, is not combative or incontinent, and does not wander, he may do well in this type of residential setting. Generally, these facilities provide the elder with support in accomplishing hygiene activities and other tasks of daily living, and offer limited opportunities for socialization and recreational activities. They offer assistance with medications as well.

If you think your parent is ready to move into one of these transitional living situations, there are some things you should do to be sure you have identified the best possible living arrangement.

- Visit several different board and care or assisted living settings. Visit not only during the day, but at night and on weekends so you can get a feel for the overall quality of care.
- Look for a facility where staff members appear to be enjoying interaction with residents.
- Observe whether meals are rushed and noisy, or whether there is an attempt to create a warm, conversational atmosphere when it is time to eat.
- Ask yourself whether the setting feels pleasant. Is it clean and neat?
- Call the health department to find out how the facility fared in its last several inspections.
- If the home or facility specializes in the care of the cognitively impaired, does it provide a secure and safe environment to accommodate walking and wandering?
- Does all the activity seem to be centered around the TV, bathing, or meal preparation, or are there special activities,

such as sing-a-longs, birthday parties, and field trips, planned on a regular basis?

Once you have addressed these areas of concern, make the choice you think you and your parent will benefit from the most. Remember that if the elder has little or no cognitive impairment, the two of you should make this choice together. You can also continue to supplement the daily special activities schedule by facilitating attendance at a day program for a day or two each week. You can also take him out with you after work and on weekends.

Assisted living can often be found in retirement centers, allowing spouses who may be at different functioning levels to both reside in the same community. These non-nursing home residential settings can cost from $800 per month to as high as you wish to pay, depending on the level of services needed and the luxury desired in the living situation. Find transitional housing by looking under "retirement homes," "assisted living," "alternative care," or "board and care" in the Yellow Pages, or call your Area Agency on Aging.

Nursing Homes

Quality of life for nursing home residents depends on a lot of factors. If all your attempts to keep your parent safe, happy, and actively productive in other settings have failed and you are considering a nursing home placement, you need to be aware of what these factors are. Factors to consider when making a nursing home placement include:

- level of emphasis on activities in the facility
- cleanliness of environment
- quality of nursing staff care
- friendliness and nondefensiveness of staff
- health department survey results, such as facility compliance with regulations regarding physical and chemical restraints (drugs), and quality and nutritional value of meals

- openness of facility staff and administration toward family involvement in facility activities and medical care
- ability of families to give input into their loved one's care, including daily schedule of activities
- staff respect of resident dignity and privacy
- staff encouragement of resident independence.

Nursing homes that crosstrain aides in activities planning and implementation, or that accomplish activities of daily living and special activities in small group settings, do a good job of providing quality-of-life experiences for their residents. (You may find this design more often on units for the cognitively impaired.) Providing a structure for the day in terms of belonging to a group and being cared for by a certain staff member builds self-esteem and a family relationship he might not have if he is simply seen as "bed 20," who needs to be bathed, taken to the toilet, or fed.

Pay close attention to the facility's activities calendar. You should get on the mailing list each month, or pick up a calendar at the activities office.

Support your parent, and the activities director, by offering to go on field trips, helping to prepare for and attending parties and other special events, or offering to lead a special activity in an area of interest to you. It will make your parent feel that you are part of his new "family" and you will also be greatly appreciated by facility staff.

Some care facilities are offering short-term respite (rest time) care. Families can place their loved one for a short period of time and later bring him or her back home.

KEEP YOUR EYES AND EARS OPEN

Senior living communities are being built all across the United States that deliver any level of care and activity support you and your parent may need. Independent living, foster care, assisted living, and nursing home care are often all available on the same campus. Research what is available in your area that might work for your parent by looking under "senior services" or "retirement communities" in the Yellow Pages, or by contacting your Area Agency on Aging.

Wherever your parent lives, whether it is in his own home, with you, or in a residential setting, look for ways to bring all his daily activities into one unified plan for keeping him happily occupied with the least possible anxiety. Whatever the setting, it should encourage your parent's participation to the fullest possible extent, in all of life's daily activities.

THINGS TO DO

√ Make a list of all the things that are important to you and your parent in choosing a living situation, such as cleanliness and location. Develop it into a working checklist that can be used as you visit residential living facilities.

√ Many caregivers are able to provide care in a home- or community-based setting for as long as their parent lives. Evaluate what factors might move you toward a nursing home placement (physical combativeness, heavy lifting, incontinence, for example). What steps can you take now that might allow your parent to keep living at home?

√ Think of special activities you may still be able to do with your parent, even after care facility placement. Keep a list of things to do and places you can go when you are together.

√ Visit a nursing home in your area. Be sure to ask about its approach to daily activities. Observe whether the residents are well cared for and happy, and whether there is a positive relationship between residents and staff.

√ Visit a day program to see how it feels as a care option. Compare it with all the other care options you may be considering for presence of warm and caring staff, how well the program fits into your work schedule, activities offered, aesthetic appeal, and any other factors that are important to you and your parent.

√ If you want to keep current on innovative day program services in area adult day centers, or if you want to start a day program in your area, write to the Robert Wood Johnson Foundation's Partners in Caregiving Project, and ask if you can begin receiving the *Dementia/Respite News.* The address is: Partners in Caregiving: The Dementia Services Program, Dept. of Psychiatry and Behavioral Medicine, Medical Center Blvd., Winston-Salem, NC 27157-1087.

√ Ask your Area Agency on Aging to send you the booklet entitled "How to Choose a Nursing Home."

GLOSSARY OF TERMS

. . . .

Activity plan. A plan developed by activity professionals with the elder who needs activity support, and often the elder's family. The activity plan supports on-going self-esteem and dignity, and personal, meaningful life activities.

Activity professionals. The people working in adult day programs, nursing homes, and retirement centers, who are responsible for providing group and one-on-one activity opportunities for residents or participants based on their wishes, their past and present interest, and on their physical and cognitive functioning levels.

ADLs (activities of daily living). These are the activities that we do every day, including such things as brushing teeth, combing hair, dressing, bathing, and eating.

Adaptive clothing. Clothing designed to help maintain a person's independence in a number of functioning areas. Examples include velcro strips in place of buttons, easy on and off features to support dressing and bathroom task accomplishment, and shoes that can be washed after soiling from incontinence.

Adult day program. A program that provides safety, activities, one to three meals per day, medical monitoring, and sometimes medical care. Often, weekend and short term overnight care is available, as well as bathing, shampoos, toenail care, and other services.

Alternative care facility. Definitions vary slightly from state to state, but generally it is a residential facility that offers assistance with medications, dressing, meals, and laundry. Nursing services are not available as part of the package. The term *alternative care facility* can be synonymous with *board and care* and *assisted living*. These types of residential facilities usually do not take severely demented people, or those with extreme wandering or combative behaviors. Some of these facilities take Medicaid, while others do not.

Alzheimer's disease. A disease characterized by progressive memory loss and confusion due to tangles and plaques that form in the brain. Short term memory is more severely affected than long term memory. The disease is progressive, lasting from two to thirty or more years.

Area Agency on Aging. An agency in a local area that administers monies from the federal government designated for the needs of aging people. Some things on which this money is spent include transportation, respite care, and nutritional services.

Assisted living. Similar to board and care or alternative care. an assisted living arrangement usually includes dressing, medications, and meals. Assisted living is often found as part of a retirement center, and sometimes at nursing homes.

Challenged. Used in this book to describe losses or disabilities older people may experience.

Continuum of care. Services that are available to the elderly and are based on their preferences and the level of care they require. The continuum may begin with in-home help from family, friends and professionals, and end with nursing home admission.

Dementia. Any condition of mental deterioration. Progressive dementia, such as Alzheimer's disease or multi-infarct dementia, cannot be reversed.

Incontinence. The state of being unable to control one's bowel and/or bladder.

In-home care. Services provided in the home including personal care services, homemaking services, and skilled nursing services.

Intergenerational activities. Activities shared by different age groups.

Long term care. A term that refers to care that takes place over a long period of time. Long term care may occur anywhere along the care continuum, although it is most often associated with nursing home care.

Multi-infarct dementia. A generally irreversible dementia caused by small strokes in the brain. If lifestyle issues that cause strokes are addressed early, progress may be slowed.

Reminiscence. To remember and discuss the past. Reminiscence represents a valuable tool in working with people who have short term memory loss. It is often it is used as an integral part of an elder's activity plan.

Sensory stimulation. An approach intended to stimulate the senses. An example discussed in this book is cooking where the elder's senses of smell, taste and touch are stimulated.

Short term memory loss. The inability to remember events that happened recently.

Word games. Games that challenge mental and cognitive abilities. A typical example would be sentence completion games ("The daring young man on the _____").

National Resource Organizations

Alzheimer's Association
919 North Michigan Avenue
Suite 1000
Chicago, IL 60611
(312) 853-3060; (800) 272-3900
(patients & families only)
The Alzheimer's Association assists family members of Alzheimer's Disease patients by offering numerous resource materials.

American Association of Homes for the Aging (AAHA)
901 E Street, NW, Suite 500
Washington, DC 20004
(202) 783-2242
A national membership organization of non-profit elderly housing organizations. AAHA offers a series of brochures on housing options for the elderly for $1.00.

American Association of Retired Persons (AARP)
601 E Street, NW
Washington, DC 20049
(202) 434-2277
AARP is a nonprofit membership organization providing a number of free publications for caregivers.

American Diabetes Association (ADA)
National Center
1660 Duke Street
Alexandria, VA 22314
(703) 549-1500; (800) 232-3472

ADA is a voluntary health organization concerned with diabetes. The association offers brochures on various topics related diabetes.

American Health Care Association (AHCA)
1201 L Street, NW
Washington, DC 20005
(202) 842-4444
(800) 321-0343 (publications only)
AHCA is an association for nursing homes. The organization distributes free brochures on selecting and paying for nursing homes.

American Parkinson Disease Association (APDA)
60 Bay Street, Suite 401
Staten Island, NY 10301
(718) 981-8001; (800) 223-2732
APDA is an association that provides information and referral, public education, and counseling on Parkinson's disease. The organization offers information and referral services for caregivers.

Catholic Charities USA
1731 King Street, #200
Alexandria, VA 22314
(703) 549-1390
Catholic Charities USA is a nationwide network that offers respite, chore services, caregiver retreats, adult day care and meals on wheels.

Center on Rural Elderly
Univ. of Missouri — Kansas City
5245 Rockhill Road
Kansas City, MO 64110
(816) 235-2180
The Center provides information and referral and self help materials to family caregivers.

Foundation for Hospice and Homecare
519 C Street, NE
Washington, DC 20002
(202) 547-6586
The Foundation offers a free publication on how to choose hospice and homecare agencies. To receive the brochure, send a stamped, self-addressed business envelope.

Health Insurance Association of America (HIAA)
1025 Connecticut Avenue, NW
Suite 1200
Washington, DC 20036
(202) 223-7780
HIAA is a membership organization for insurance companies. The association offers free publications on how to evaluate long term care and Medigap insurance policies.

Medic Alert Foundation International
2323 Colorado Avenue
Turlock, CA 95380
(209) 669-2402; (800) 344-3226
The Foundation offers personal emergency response systems and medical alert bracelets and neck chains.

National Academy of Elder Law Attorneys
655 N. Alvernon Way, Suite 108
Tucson, AZ 84711
(602) 881-4005
The Academy is membership organization for elder law attorneys. It offers a free brochure on how to choose an elder law attorney.

National Association of Activity Professionals
1225 I Street, NW, Suite 300
Washington, DC 20005
(202) 289-0722
NAAP is an association for professionals working in nursing homes, senior centers, retirement housing, and adult day care programs. Other interested individuals are invited. They offer an annual convention, continuing education programs, and a monthly newsletter.

National Association of Private Geriatric Care Managers
655 N. Alvernon Way, Suite 108
Tucson, AZ 86711
(602) 881-8008
NAPGCM is an association of private practitioners who provide care management services for the elderly.

National Association on Area Agencies on Aging (N4A)
1112 16th Street, NW, Suite 100
Washington, DC 20036
(202) 296-8130; (800) 677-1116
(Eldercare Locator Service)

N4A is a membership organization for the 670 Area Agencies on Aging across the country. It offers the Eldercare Locator Service, a nationwide service to help caregivers find community services for the elderly.

National Council on the Aging
409 Third Street, SW
Washington, DC 20024
(202) 479-1200
NCOA is a national , nonprofit membership organization. It offers a number of useful publications for caregivers.

National Institute on Aging (NIA)
9000 Rockville Pike
Bethesda, MD 20892
(301) 496-4000
The NIA, part of the National Institutes on Health, is a federal government's principal agency that distributes free resource materials including a series of fact sheets on aging, called *Age Pages*.

National Stroke Association
300 East Hampden Avenue,
Suite 240
Englewood, CO 80110
(303) 762-9922; (800) 787-6537
The National Stroke Association publishes a number of brochures to help family members cope with stroke patients.

The Simon Foundation
P.O. Box 815
Wilmette, IL 60091
(708) 864-3913; (800) 237-4666
(patient information)
The Simon Foundation provides public education on incontinence.

United Parkinson Foundation
360 West Superior Street
Chicago, IL 60610
(312) 664-2344
The United Parkinson Foundation offers educational symposia for Parkinson patients and their families.

Vision Foundation, Inc.
818 Mt. Auburn Street
Watertown, MA 02172
(617) 926-4232; (800) 852-3029 (Massachusetts only)
The Foundation provides self-help services to individuals and their families coping with vision impairments.

Visiting Nurse Associations of America (VNAA)
3801 East Florida Avenue
Suite 206
Denver, CO 80210
(303) 753-0218; (800) 426-2547 (referral line)
VNAA offers a toll-free number for family members and professionals to locate a Visiting Nurses Association in their area.

Further Reading

Note: Some of the books listed below, especially those published by The Haworth Press and Springer Publishing Company, are intended for gerontologists and other healthcare professionals. Some readers may therefore find them to be too technical and specific for their needs.

Beisgen, Beverly Ann
Life Enhancing Activities for Mentally Impaired Elders: A Practical Guide. New York: Springer Publishing Co., 1989.

Budge, Meredith
A Wealth of Experience: A Guide to Activities for Older People. Philadelphia: F.A. Davis Company, 1989.

Coberly, Lenore M., Jeri McCormick, and Karen Updike
Writers Have No Age: Creative Writing with Older Adults. Binghamton, NY: The Haworth Press, 1985.

Crepeau, Elizabeth L.
Activities Programming. Surham, NH: New England Gerontology Center, 1980.

Cunninghis, Richelle N.
Reality Activities: A How-to Manual for Use with Confused and Disoriented Elderly. Bradenton Beach, FL: Geriatric Educational Consultants, 1982.

DeBolt, Nancy and Mary Ellen Kastner
I'm in Here! Strategies for One-to-One Activities. Torrington, WY: Lutheran Health Systems, 1989.

Flatten Kay, Barbara Wilhite, and Eleanor Reys-Watson
Exercise Activities for the Elderly. New York: Springer Publishing Company, 1988.

Recreation Activities for the Elderly. New York: Springer Publishing Company, 1988.

Foster, Phyllis M.
Therapeutic Activities with the Impaired Elderly. Binghamton, NY: The Haworth Press, 1986.

Activities and the "Well Elderly". Binghamton, NY: The Haworth Press, 1983.

Freeman, Sally
Activities and Approaches for Alzheimers. Knoxville, TN: Whitfield Agency, 1987.

Glickstein, Joan K.
Therapeutic Interventions in Alzheimer's Disease: A Program of Functional Communication Skills for Activities of Daily Living. Rockville, MD: Aspen Publishers, 1988.

Hauser, Roger L.
Activities with Senior Adults. Nashville, TN: Broadman Press, 1991.

Hegelson, Elsbeth M. and Scott C. Willis
Handbook of Group Activities for Impaired Older Adults. Binghamton, NY: The Haworth Press, 1987.

Keller, M. Jean, editor
Activities with Developmentally Disabled Elderly & Older Adults. Binghamton, NY: The Haworth Press, 1990.

Lowman, Evelyn
Arts and Crafts for the Elderly: A Resource Book for Activity Directors in Healthcare Facilities. New York: Springer Publishing Company, 1992.

McGuire, Francis A., Rosangela K. Boyd, and Ann James, editors.
Therapeutic Humor with the Elderly. Binghamton, NY: The Haworth Press, 1993.

McMurray, Janice
Creative Arts with Older People. Binghamton, NY: The Haworth Press, 1989.

Parker, Sandra D. and Carol Will
Activities for the Elderly, Vol.2: Programming for Individuals with Significant Impairments. Ravensdale, WA: Idyll Arbor, Inc., 1993.

Parker, Sandra D., Carol Will, and Cheryl L. Burke
Activities for the Elderly, Vol. 1: A Guide to Quality Programming. Ravensdale, WA: Idyll Arbor, Inc., 1989.

Sheridan, Carmel
Reminiscence: Uncovering a Lifetime of Memories. San Francisco: ElderPress, 1991.

Failure-free Activities for the Alzheimer's Patient: A Guidebook for Caregivers. San Francisco: Cottage Books, 1987.

Sessoms, Robert L.
One-Hundred Fifty Ideas for Activities with Senior Adults. Nashville, TN: Broadman Press, 1977.

Thurman, Anne and Carol Ann Piggins
Drama Activities with Older Adults: A Handbook for Leaders. New York: The Haworth Press, 1982.

Williams, Janice L. and Janet Downs
Educational Activity Programs for Older Adults. Binghamton, NY: The Haworth Press, 1984.

Zgola, Jitka M.
Doing Things: A Guide to Programming Activities for Persons with Alzheimer's Disease and Related Disorders. Baltimore: Johns Hopkins University Press, 1987.

Other Resources

Bi Folkal Productions, Inc.
809 Williamson Street, Madison, WI 53703
Phone: (608) 251-2818, Fax: (608) 251-2874

Bi Folkal offers cassettes of old time radio favorites, as well as activity kits designed around certain holidays or special events. (For a listing of more than 49,000 cassette titles, ask your librarian for the publication, Words on Cassette, published by R.R. Bowker.)

Center for the Study of Aging, Serif Press, Inc.
1331 H Street NW, Washington, DC 20005
Phone: (202) 737-4650, order line: (800) 221-4272

This company publishes a catalog which lists hundreds of aging-related books and audio and video tapes.

Golden Horizons, Inc.
PO Box 193, Sullivan, IL 61951
Phone: (217) 728-8182

Their materials are designed to support activity professionals in care facilities, but many ideas and resources will also be helpful for family caregivers.

Elder Games
11710 Hunters Lane, Rockville, MD 20852
Phone: (301) 984-8336, order line: (800) 637-2604

Elder Games offers a large number of activity resources, including ideas for both physical and mental stimulation.

American Association of Retired Persons (AARP)
AARP Program Resource Department
PO Box 19269, Station R, Washington, DC 20036

Write to the above address and request the two publications, Activities with Impact *and* Growing Together: An Intergenerational Sourcebook. *Both publications have excellent information on intergenerational activities and physical exercises.*

G. K. Hall & Co.
70 Lincoln Street, Boston, MA 02111
Phone: (617) 423--3990, toll-free (800) 343-2806

Thorndike Press
PO Box 159, Thorndike, ME 04986
(207) 948-2962

These two companies both publish large print books, including current best sellers.

Potentials Development
775 Main Street, Suite 604, Buffalo, NY 14203
(716) 842-2658

This company shares a wide variety of activity ideas, from music and exercise to reminiscence and games.

For further activity resources, see pages 78 and 93 in this book.

INDEX

ABOUT THE AUTHOR

Susan Walker is Manager of the DayBreak Adult Day Program, Seniors' Resource Center of Jefferson County, Wheat Ridge, Colorado. She is past President of the Denver Metro Chapter of the Colorado Activity Professionals' Association, on the HCBS Advisory Council for the State of Colorado, and Chair of the Colorado Association of Homes and Services for the Aging (CAHSA) Adult Day Care Providers Group, as well as a CAHSA board member. DayBreak was recently honored by being named one of 50 national demonstration sites by the Robert Wood Johnson Foundation Partners in Caregiving Program. Ms. Walker acts as Project Director for the site.

ADVISORY PANEL MEMBERS

The following individuals reviewed working drafts of this book to assure currency, accuracy and appropriateness for the general reading public.

· · · · · · · · · ·

Nancy E. DeBolt, B.A., ACC, is a writer, speaker, consultant, and practitioner in the field of activities in the long-term care setting. She co-authored the activity guide, *I'm In Here! Strategies for One-to-One Activities*, which is now in its fifth printing. She is the LIFE Resources Consultant at Goshen Care Center, Torrington, Wyoming, where she has been involved in activities and social services for ten years. Nancy is past president of the Wyoming Activity Coordinators' Association, and has been on the board of the National Association of Activity Professionals since 1990.

Phyllis M. Foster, ACC, has recently retired as Therapeutic Activities Consultant to a number of long-term care facilities. She is the Editor of the professional journal, *Activities, Adaptation & Aging*, and has many years experience in the field of aging and activities. Ms. Foster has served as President of the National Association of Activity Professionals and in various leadership positions in the Colorado Activity Professionals' Association. She is currently a member of the Older Women's League, Denver chapter.

Sister John Antonio Miller, C.PP.S., a member of the Sisters of the Most Precious Blood of O'fallon, Missouri, is the Founder/Administrator of St. Elizabeth Adult Day Care Centers in St. Louis, Missouri. She has a master's degree in gerontology and health services management. She is a member of the advisory board of the Barnes Hospital Home Health Agency; St. Louis

University School of Medicine, Division of Geriatric Psychiatry Advisory Board; and the Alzheimer's Association Speakers Bureau. Sister is extremely interested in Quality Improvement issues in the provision of community based long-term care.

Ruth Perschbacher, ACC, RMT-BC, is the owner of Bristlecone Consulting Company. She consults to long-term care facilities and employee assistance programs on a variety of aging issues. Ms. Perschbacher serves on the Federal Assessment Advisory Committee for nursing homes and is the author of many articles and position papers on quality of life for nursing home residents. She also maintains a private practice in music therapy in Asheville, North Carolina.

Marian P. Smith, ACC, is a certified activity consultant in long-term care. She is presently semiretired and devotes much of her time to writing, lecturing, and volunteering in the field of aging. She is a pioneer in activities programming in Colorado, having been instrumental in establishing the Colorado Activity Professionals Association and promoting and participating in the education of activity personnel since 1963.

Robbyn R. Wacker, Ph.D., is an Assistant Professor at the University of Northern Colorado in the Gerontology program. In addition to teaching courses in gerontology, she has published and lectured on later life families, health behaviors in later life, and legal issues of concern to older adults. She currently serves as a board member of the Eldergarden Adult Day Program in Greeley, Colorado.

ORDER FORM

American Source Books/Impact Publishers, Inc.
P.O. Box 1094
San Luis Obispo, CA 93406
Phone orders: 1-800-2-IMPACT

Please send the following books to:

Name _____

Address _____

City/State/Zip _____

Qty	Book	Price	Total
	Caring for Your Aging Parents	8.95	
	Long Distance Caregiving	9.95	
	Care Log (caregiver workbook)	14.95	
	Keeping Active	8.95	

☐ *CHECK ENCLOSED (payable to American Source Books)*
(Total from above plus $2.50 postage for the first book and 50¢
for each additional book)

☐ *CREDIT CARD PURCHASE*

Card Number _____

Expiration Date _____

Signature X _____

☐ I do not wish to order now but please put me on your mailing
list so I can receive information on future books in *The Working
Caregiver Series.*

What Reviewers have to say about the first two books in

— *THE WORKING CAREGIVER SERIES* —

Caring for Your Aging Parents, by Kerri Smith

"This is the first book to offer a firm balance between psychological concerns and practical caregiving routines."
— *The Midwest Book Review*

"A very practical how-to-do-it manual for caregivers...full of excellent information, written in a very readable style...like having a coach, guide and friend praising, encouraging, and helping you every step of the way."
— *The CAPSULE*, CAPS (Children of Aging Parents)

"*Caring for Your Aging Parent*s has the most useful, sensible information on this subject that I've seen. Furthermore it is succinctly written and it is rooted in common sense."
— Prof. Harry James Cargas, KWMU, Missouri Public Radio

"I found this book an absolute delight in terms of providing realistic information coupled with creative strategies...I recommend it for both family members and care managers."
— Pat Percival, LCSW, *Inside GCM* (Nat'l Assn of Professional Geriatric Care Managers)

Long Distance Caregiving, by Angela Heath

"Detailed coverage of how to organize, sustain, and monitor care for an elderly parent or relative...Its organizational suggestions are excellent and badly needed..."
— *Booklist* (American Library Association)

"...written in a succinct manner—perfect for the harried caregiver."
— Marcie Parker, *Geriatric Care Management Journal*

"Heath's volume is precise, concise, and a helpful introduction to one who is new to the art of caregiving and wishes to succeed in that art!"
— Catherine F. Siffin, Indiana Univ. Center on Aging and Aged

"There is solid information in *Long Distance Caregiving*...This small, extensively researched book may save the sanity of anyone whose responsibilities include caring for another, near or far."
— *Small Press*